The Retirement Researcher's Guide Series

Reverse Mortgages

How to Use Reverse Mortgages
to Secure Your Retirement

Second Edition

Wade D. Pfau,
Ph.D., CFA

The Retirement Researcher's Guide Series
Reverse Mortgages
How to Use Reverse Mortgages to Secure Your Retirement
Second Edition
Wade D. Pfau, PhD, CFA

Library of Congress Cataloging-in-Publication Data:
Pfau, Wade, 1977–
   Reverse Mortgages: How to Use Reverse Mortgages to Secure Your Retirement / Wade Pfau.
   pages cm
   Includes index.
ISBN [978-1-945640-04-9] (paperback) - ISBN [978-1-945640-05-6] (ebook)

Library of Congress Control Number:
Retirement Researcher Media, McLean, VIRGINIA

1. Retirement Planning. 2. Financial, Personal. I. Title.

Cover design: Mineral Interactive
Graphics and Layout: Watermark Design Services
Printed in the United States of America

To my growing family.

TABLE OF CONTENTS

PREFACE (SECOND EDITION)

All of this may sound too good to be true, and it probably is to some extent. Perhaps this is why it is difficult to grasp the concept of line of credit growth throughout retirement. I've already noted that unused lines of credit work for borrowers to the detriment of lenders and the government insurance fund. Such use of a reverse mortgage still exists today and would be contractually protected for those who initiate reverse mortgages under the current rules. At some point in the future, I expect to see new limitations about line of credit growth, especially as more people start to follow the findings of recent research on this matter.

Line of credit growth may be viewed a bit like an unintended loophole that is strengthened by our low interest rate environment. The rules will probably be changed someday for newly issued loans. Until then, research points to this growth as a valuable way reverse mortgages can contribute to a retirement income plan.

—From the first edition of this book, page 72

And so it goes with government-administered programs: financial planners use their acumen to find uses and strategies that government policymakers do not anticipate. It happened with Social Security in November 2015, when sophisticated Social Security-claim strategies were phased out in response to financial planners catching on about how to obtain additional spousal benefits from the program. And it happened with reverse mortgages in October 2017, because financial planners had seen how setting up a growing line of credit with the Home Equity Conversion Mortgage (HECM) program offered invaluable options for building more efficient retirement-income plans.

On August 29, 2017, the Department of Housing and Urban Development (HUD) announced new rules effective on October 2, 2017 that reduce some of the momentum and value from reverse-mortgage line of credit uses. Under the new regime, it will be a tougher psychological hurdle to pull the trigger on opening a reverse mortgage before it is needed, in order to let the line of credit grow. Up-front costs will be higher, primarily because of an increased initial mortgage-insurance premium, and the line of credit will grow more slowly and from a lower initial base. For those who initiated reverse mortgages prior to October 2, the old rules still apply, and the first edition of the book still provides the correct details about how their reverse mortgages will operate. This book is for readers thinking about opening a reverse mortgage after October 2, 2017.

Not all is lost, though, for those who did not get their applications for a reverse mortgage submitted by that October 2017 deadline. Though the initial costs of setting up a reverse mortgage will be higher due to a larger initial mortgage-insurance premium and the growth for the line of credit will be less due to a lower initial borrowing amount and a smaller ongoing mortgage-insurance premium, the line of credit still remains as a viable option and use for a reverse mortgage. In this new edition, I will fully update all of the original analyses from the first edition to account for the current rules.

Nonetheless, setting up lines of credit for future use was never the most popular way to use a reverse mortgage. People generally open reverse mortgages because they wish to spend the proceeds sooner rather than later. Refinancing a traditional mortgage into a reverse mortgage to reduce the fixed payments in the early years of retirement has been the most popular use for a HECM reverse mortgage. Arguably, the new rules have made using a reverse mortgage in this way more attractive, especially when the remaining mortgage to be refinanced is a larger percentage of the available reverse-mortgage proceeds.

More generally, as a part of revising this book for the new October 2017 rules, I've changed my emphasis a bit away from reverse mortgage uses that open a line of credit for distant potential uses and toward using a reverse mortgage to spend the proceeds more quickly, such as by refinancing a traditional mortgage, purchasing a new home with the HECM for Purchase, and building a bridge to help support the ability to delay Social Security benefits to age seventy.

As well, when it comes to coordinating retirement spending with a reverse mortgage, results in the first edition suggested that the most effective way to do so was to open a line of credit as early as possible but to spend from it only in the event that the portfolio is depleted. In this new edition, emphasis shifts toward more coordinated strategies that draw from the reverse mortgage throughout retirement. These coordinated strategies now have a greater benefit, because some of the value of just letting a line of credit grow endlessly before using it has now been diminished.

Briefly, the new reverse-mortgage rules implemented in October 2017 include:

- The initial-mortgage insurance premium when opening a reverse mortgage is now 2 percent of the home value up to the $679,650 (as of January 1, 2018, and subject to change) lending limit. This has changed from a previous dueling-premium approach that depended on the amount borrowed in the first year; it was 0.5 percent if less than 60 percent of the allowed borrowing amountwas taken in the first year and 2.5 percent if more than 60 percent of the allowed borrowing amount was taken in the first year.
- The ongoing mortgage-insurance premium on the loan balance has been reduced to 0.5 percent from the previous 1.25 percent.
- A new table of principal limit factors was issued, and these generally result in a reduced initial borrowing amount with the reverse mortgage, at least when interest rates are low.
- The floor on the expected rate used to calculate initial borrowing amounts on a reverse mortgage was reduced from 5.06 percent to 3 percent, which does have some interesting implications in our low-interest-rate environment.

In addition to updating the book's coverage for these new rules, I've also expanded the research around different uses for a reverse mortgage. In the second edition, deeper coverage and simulations are also provided for the following reverse-mortgage uses:

- Refinancing an existing mortgage at the start of retirement, with the possibility of also making voluntary repayments to the reverse-mortgage loan balance.
- Considering the HECM for Purchase alongside other options for purchasing a new home at the start of retirement.
- Using a reverse mortgage to fill in for the missing early Social Security benefits when delaying Social Security to age seventy.

I continue to welcome your feedback and questions.

You can reach me at wade@retirementresearcher.com.

Wade Pfau
Bryn Mawr, PA
January 2018

PREFACE (FIRST EDITION)

Reverse mortgages are an important tool in the retirement-income toolkit. As a professor of retirement income, I meant to investigate them more carefully for a long time. I suppose they did not quickly rise to the top of my to-do list because of the conventional wisdom that they are generally not a very good tool. In the fall of 2014, I began focusing more on them and quickly found them to be a fascinating and misunderstood financial product.

As I began writing about reverse mortgages, I only had in mind the idea of creating a resource that could serve as a chapter in a larger retirement-income book. At some point, I realized I was developing something that could serve as an entire book on the subject. It has been a lot of fun to conduct original research and write about how reverse mortgages can fit into a retirement-income plan. Using reverse mortgages to improve sustainability for a responsible retirement plan is still a relatively new and unexplored area of consideration. Research on the subject began in earnest only in 2012, and the government's modifications since 2013 to the Home Equity Conversion Mortgage program have also pushed public policy in this direction.

I hope this book will serve as a good resource with unbiased information for individuals who are considering a reverse mortgage for their financial plans. Most reverse mortgage books are written by those who originate loans. This is not to say that such authors cannot provide an unbiased presentation on the subject, but readers can be confident that I do not receive any financial gain from the sale of reverse mortgages. I am writing from outside the reverse mortgage industry. My overarching interest is in building efficient retirement-income plans. My research has led me to conclude that in many cases, reverse mortgages can provide value toward achieving this end, and this is the goal of my writing. I hope you will find this exploration of the research useful.

I welcome your feedback and questions.

You can reach me at wade@retirementresearcher.com.

As a final note, I have tried to avoid including footnotes to make the book more readable and give it a less academic feel. The end of each chapter includes a list for "further reading" that includes the bibliographic information for resources mentioned within the chapter.

Wade Pfau
Bryn Mawr, PA
September 2016

ACKNOWLEDGEMENTS

Writing a book is a major endeavor, and countless individuals have helped me along the way by. First and foremost, I would like to thank my colleagues at McLean Asset Management for providing the vision and resources to make this book possible. In particular, I'm grateful for the leadership and willingness of Alex Murguia and Dean Umemoto to build a firm that can turn my research on retirement-income planning into practical solutions for real-world retirees. I would also like to thank the entire advisory team at McLean: Kevin Brawner, Athena Chang, Rob Cordeau, Jason Dye, Bob French, Paula Friedman, Joel Gemmell, Christian Litscher, Kyle Meyer, Robert Papa, Mark Witaschek, and Jessica Wunder.

I am also deeply indebted to Don and Lynne Komai and the Watermark Design Office for their assistance in developing the layout and design for this book. The team at Mineral Interactive has also provided invaluable help in preparing this book. Thank you to Jud Mackrill, Kim Mackrill, Zach McDonald, Johnny Sandquist, Rebecca Tschetter, and everyone else there who has made a contribution.

Furthermore, I am grateful to The American College of Financial Services for its leadership and focus on retirement-income planning, particularly Bob Johnson, Michael Finke, David Littell, and Jamie Hopkins.

Next, thank you to Shelley Giordano and the Funding Longevity Taskforce (Barry Sacks, Marguerita Cheng, Thomas C. B. Davison, Christopher Mayer, John Salter, and Sandra Timmermann) for introducing me to and educating me about reverse mortgages, and for being a resource to answer my many questions as I've written on this subject. Extra thanks to Tom Davison for suggesting the book title and providing me with detailed comments on my draft.

The next group of individuals I must thank include many reverse-mortgage professionals who have helped me better understand their industry. These include, in alphabetical order, Harlan Accola, Marvis Baehr, Peter Bell, Chuck Berry, Jim Cullen, Joe Damo, Tom Dickson, Don Graves, Christina Harmes, Dan Hultquist, Tim Jackson, Todd Jarvis, Darryl Johnson, Elena Katsulos, Vaughn Kavlie, Joe DeMarkey, Rasty Goodwin, Mary Lafaye, Bob Mikelskas, Christian Mills, Scott Norman, Alex Pistone, Colleen Rideout, Jim Spicka, James Stanko, Robert Trommler, James Veale, Jim Warns, and Jenny Werwa.

When it comes to retirement-income planning, I wish to thank countless other individuals. A partial list must include Dana Anspach, David Blanchett, J. Brent Burns, Curtis Cloke, Jeremy Cooper, Dirk Cotton, Harold Evensky, Francois Gadenne, Robert Huebscher, Stephen Huxley, Michael Kitces, Manish Malhoutra, Betty Meredith, Moshe Milevsky, Aaron Minney, Dan Moisand, Robert Powell, Dick Purcell, Joe Tomlinson, Steve Vernon, and the editorial team at the Journal of Financial Planning.

Finally, I wish to thank everyone who has read and participated at my blog and website, RetirementResearcher.com.

CHAPTER 1

Overview of Retirement Income Planning

Without the relative stability provided by earnings from employment, retirees must find a way to convert their financial resources into a stream of income that will last the remainder of their lives. Two trends add to the difficulty of this task. First, people are living longer, and those retiring in their sixties must plan to support a longer period of spending. Second, traditional defined-benefit pensions are becoming less common. Pensions once guaranteed lifetime income by pooling risks across a large number of workers, but fewer employees have access to them today. Instead, employees and employers now tend to contribute to various defined-contribution pensions like 401(k)s, where the employee accepts longevity and investment risk and must make investment decisions. 401(k) plans are not pensions in the traditional sense, as they shift the risks and responsibilities to employees.

If you've been saving and accumulating, the question remains about what to do with your pot of assets on reaching retirement. Essentially, if you wish to retire one day, you are increasingly responsible to figure out how to save during your working years and convert your savings into sustainable income for an ever-lengthening number of retirement years. It is not an easy task, but it is manageable.

My goal is to help guide you along the right path to building an efficient retirement-income strategy. This book focuses on home equity and whether it may be worthwhile to include a reverse mortgage in one's retirement-income toolkit. Ultimately, this is something that you, as an informed consumer of the financial-services profession, may seek to do on your own, but I will also offer suggestions on how to obtain further assistance if you decide to seek it.

It is important to note from the outset that retirement-income planning is still a relatively new field. Wealth management has traditionally focused on accumulating assets without applying further thought to the differences between pre- and postretirement financial risk. To put it succinctly, retirees experience a reduced capacity to bear financial-market risk compared to when they still earned income. The standard of living for a retiree becomes more vulnerable to enduring permanent harm as a result of financial-market downturns.

While it is relatively new, retirement-income planning has emerged as a distinct field in the financial-services profession. It continues to suffer from growing pains as it gains recognition, but increased research and brainpower in the field have benefited those planning for retirement and current retirees alike. It is now clear that the financial circumstances facing retirees are not the same as those of preretirees, calling for different approaches from traditional investment advice for wealth accumulation. Reverse mortgages may seem an odd vehicle when considered with an accumulation mind-set, but they can make sense in a retirement-income framework.

A mountain-climbing analogy is useful for clarifying the distinction between accumulation and distribution: the ultimate goal of climbing a mountain is not just to make it to the top; it is also necessary to get back

Exhibit 1.1

The Mountain Climbing Analogy for Retirement

down. And the skill set required to get down a mountain is not the same as that needed to reach the summit. In fact, an experienced mountain climber knows that going back down is more treacherous and dangerous, because climbers must deal with greater fatigue, they risk falling farther and with greater acceleration when facing a downslope compared to an upslope, and the way our bodies are designed makes going up easier than coming down.

Distribution—the retirement phase when you are pulling money from your accounts rather than accumulating wealth—is much like descending a mountain. So, the objective of a retirement saver is not just to make it to the top of the mountain (achieve a wealth-accumulation target). The real objective is to safely and smoothly make it down the mountain, spending assets in a sustainable manner for as long as you live. When viewed in this retirement-income context, the potential role and value of a reverse mortgage might make more sense than when one is still thinking within a typical accumulation mind-set.

◎ The Retirement-Researcher Manifesto

As I have attempted to summarize the key messages and themes that have underscored the writing and research I have put into this book, I've found that the following eight guidelines may serve as a manifesto for my approach to retirement-income planning. Much of my writing concerns how to implement these guidelines into a retirement-income plan.

1. Play the long game. You should base your retirement-income strategy on planning to live, not planning to die. A long life will be expensive to support, and it should take precedence over death planning. Fight the impatience that could lead you to choose short-term expediencies that carry greater long-term cost. This does not mean, however, that you must sacrifice short-term satisfactions to plan for the long term. Many efficiencies can be gained from a long-term focus that can sustain a higher standard of living for as long as you live.

You still have to plan for a long life, even when rejecting strategies that only help in the event of a long life. Remember, planning for average life expectancy is quite risky—by definition, half of the population outlives it. Planning to live longer means spending less than otherwise. Developing a plan that incorporates efficiencies that will not be realized until later can allow more spending today in anticipation of those efficiencies. Not taking such long-term, efficiency-improving actions will lead to a permanently reduced standard of living.

Some examples of focusing on the long-term plan over accepting short-term expediencies include:

- delaying the start of Social Security benefits,
- purchasing income annuities,
- paying a bit more taxes today in order to enjoy more substantial tax reductions in the future,
- making home renovations and living arrangements with the idea of aging in place,
- planning for the risk of cognitive decline that will make it harder to manage your finances with age,
- developing an estate plan, and
- opening a line of credit with a reverse mortgage.

These strategies may not make much sense if the planning horizon is only a couple of years, but they may make a great deal of sense for someone building a sustainable long-term retirement-income plan.

2. Do not leave money on the table. The holy grail of retirement-income planning is a set of strategies that enhance retirement efficiency. I define efficiency this way: if one strategy simultaneously allows for more lifetime spending and a greater legacy value for assets relative to another strategy, then it is more efficient. Efficiency must be defined from the perspective of how long you live.

Related to point (1), there can be a number of strategies that enhance efficiency over the long term (but not necessarily over the short term) with more spending and more legacy. One simple example for tax planning in retirement is taking IRA distributions or harvesting capital gains to generate enough income to fill the 0 percent marginal tax bracket.

3. Use reasonable expectations for portfolio returns. A key lesson for long-term financial planning is that you should not expect to earn the average historical market returns for your portfolio. Half of the time, realized returns will be less. As well, we have been experiencing a period of historically low interest rates, which unfortunately provides a clear mathematical reality that at least bond returns are going to be lower in the future. This has important implications for those who have retired (they are relevant for those far from retirement as well, but the harm of ignoring them is less than for retirees). At the very least, dismiss any retirement projection based on 8 percent or 12 percent returns, as the reality is likely much less when we account for portfolio volatility, inflation, a desire to develop a plan that will work more than half the time, and with today's low interest rates. As a corollary to this point, while low interest rates generally make retirement more expensive, there are some strategies that are made more attractive by low interest rates, such as delaying Social Security or opening a reverse mortgage.

4. *Be careful about plans that only work with high market returns.* A natural mathematical formula that applies to retirement planning is that higher assumed future market returns imply higher sustainable spending rates. Bonds provide a fixed rate of return when held to maturity, and stocks potentially offer a higher return than bonds as a reward for their additional risk. But a "risk premium" is not guaranteed and may not materialize. Retirees who spend more today because they are planning for higher market returns than available for bonds are essentially "amortizing their upside." They are spending more today than justified by bond investments, based on an assumption that higher returns in the future will make up the difference and justify the higher spending rate.

For retirees, the fundamental nature of risk is the threat that poor market returns trigger a permanently lower standard of living. Retirees must decide how much risk to their lifestyle they are willing to accept. Assuming that a risk premium on stocks will be earned and spending more today is risky behavior. It may be reasonable behavior for the more risk tolerant among us, but it is not an appropriate behavior for everyone. It is important to think through the consequences in advance.

5. *Build an integrated strategy to manage various retirement risks.* A good retirement-income strategy combines the best retirement-income tools for meeting one's goals while protecting against risk. Such risks include an unknown planning horizon due to longevity; market volatility and macroeconomic risks; and inflation and spending shocks that can derail

a budget. Manage these risks by combining income tools with different relative strengths and weaknesses for addressing each of them.

6. *Approach retirement-income tools with an agnostic view.* The financial-services profession generally divides into two camps of focus: one on investment solutions and one on insurance solutions. Both sides have adherents who see little use for the other side. But the most efficient retirement strategies integrate both solutions. It is potentially harmful to dismiss subsets of retirement-income tools without a thorough investigation of their purported role. In this regard, it is wrong to describe the stock market as a "casino," to lump income annuities with every other type of annuity, and to dismiss reverse mortgages without any further consideration.

For either camp of the financial-services profession, it is natural to accuse its opposite of having conflicts of interest that bias its advice, but each side must consider whether this is true of itself. A natural conflict for an insurance agent is receiving commission for selling insurance products that meet the sole requirement that they are "suitable" for the client. On the investments side, those charging a percentage of the assets they manage naturally wish to make investment portfolios as large as possible, which is not necessarily in the best interest of clients, who are seeking sustainable lifetime income and proper retirement-risk management. Meanwhile, those charging hourly fees for planning advice naturally prefer to avoid recommendations so simple that clients don't see the need for ongoing planning relationships. It is important to overcome these hurdles and to rely carefully on what the math and research show. This requires starting from a fundamentally agnostic position.

7. *Start by assessing all household assets and liabilities.* The retirement balance sheet is the starting point for building a retirement-income strategy; a retirement plan involves more than just financial assets. This has been a fundamental lesson from various retirement frameworks such as Jason Branning and M. Ray Grubbs's Modern Retirement Theory, Russell Investments' funded-ratio approach, and the household balance-sheet view of the Retirement Income Industry Association.

At the core of these different methodologies is a desire to treat the household retirement problem in the same way that pension funds treat their obligations. Assets should be matched to liabilities with comparable levels of risk. This can be done either on a balance-sheet level, using the present values of asset and liability streams, or on a period-by-period basis to match assets to ongoing spending needs. Structuring the retirement-income problem in this way makes it easier to keep track of the different aspects of the plan and to make sure that each liability has a funding source. This also allows retirees to more easily determine whether they have sufficient assets to meet their retirement needs or if they may be underfunded with respect to their goals. This organizational framework also serves as a foundation for deciding on an appropriate asset allocation and for seeing clearly how different retirement-income tools fit into an overall plan. It also pushes us to think beyond just the investment portfolio and to more deeply contemplate how substantial assets like home equity can best fit into an overall plan.

Exhibit 1.2 provides a basic overview of potential assets and liabilities to consider.

Basic Household Assets and Liabilities

Assets	Liabilities
Human Capital • Continuing career • Part-time work	Fixed Expenses • Basic living needs • Taxes • Debt repayment
Home Equity	
Financial Assets • Checking accounts • Brokerage accounts • Retirement plans	Discretionary Expenses • Travel & leisure • Lifestyle improvements
Insurance & Annuities	Contingencies • Long-Term care • Health care • Other spending shocks
Social Capital • Social security • Medicare • Company pensions • Family & community	Legacy Goals • Family • Community & society

Exhibit 1.2

8. Distinguish between technical liquidity and true liquidity. An important implication of the retirement balance-sheet view is that the nature of liquidity in a retirement-income plan must be carefully considered. In a sense, an investment portfolio is a liquid asset, but some of its liquidity may be only an illusion. Assets must be matched to liabilities. Some, or even all, of the investment portfolio may be earmarked to meet future lifestyle spending goals. Curtis Cloke describes this in his Thrive University program for financial advisors (which I have attended twice) as *allocation liquidity*. Retirees are free to reallocate their assets in any way they wish, but the assets are not as liquid as they appear, because they must be preserved to meet the spending goal. In other words, while a retiree could decide to use these assets for another purpose, doing so would jeopardize the ability to meet future spending.

This is different from free-spending liquidity, in which assets can be spent in any desired way because they are not earmarked to meet existing liabilities. True liquidity applies only to excess assets remaining after setting aside what is needed to meet all household liabilities. This distinction is important, because tying up part of one's assets in something illiquid, such as an income annuity, may allow for household liabilities to be covered more cheaply than when all assets are positioned to provide technical liquidity. In simple terms, an income annuity that pools longevity risk may allow lifetime spending to be met at a cost of twenty years of the spending objective, while self-funding for longevity may require setting aside enough from an investment portfolio to cover thirty to forty years of expenses.

Because risk pooling and mortality credits allow for less to be set aside to cover the spending goal, there is now greater true liquidity and therefore more to cover other unexpected contingencies without jeopardizing core spending needs. Liquidity, as it is traditionally defined in securities markets, is of little value as a distinct goal in a long-term retirement-income plan.

◎ The Retirement-Income Challenge

As we've noted, A good retirement-income strategy combines the best retirement-income tools for meeting one's goals while protecting against risk. Building an optimal strategy is a process, and there is no single right answer. No one approach or retirement-income product works best for everyone. Different people will approach the problem in different ways. Some will prefer to manage withdrawals from an investment portfolio, while others will prefer to build income guarantees. The objective is to flesh out the details of how each income tool could contribute, quantify the advantages and disadvantages of different strategies, and determine how to best combine the income tools into an overall plan.

Exhibit 1.3 shows the retirement-income planning problem as a series of concentric circles. I call it the "retirement-income challenge." The innermost circle summarizes the overall process for retirement income. At the center, we must combine income tools to best meet goals and balance risks.

Possible goals are listed in the next concentric circle. The third circle lists risks confronting those goals. The final outside circle shows available income tools for building a retirement-income plan.

Financial Goals for Retirement

It is important to clarify the goals for a retirement-income plan, as different income tools are better suited for different goals. Retirement plans should be customized to each person's specific circumstances. Each retiree should seek to meet specific financial goals in a way that best manages the wide variety of risks that threaten those goals. The primary financial goal for most retirees relates to their spending: maximize spending power (lifestyle) in such a way that at least core expenses can

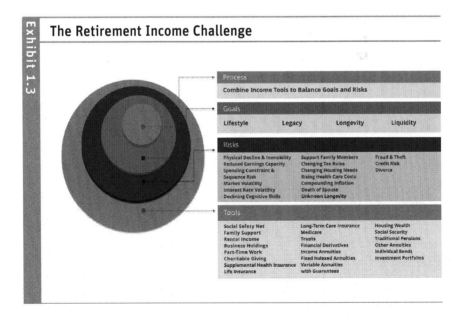

The Retirement Income Challenge

be met sustainably without any drastic reductions, no matter how long the retirement lasts (longevity). Other important goals may include leaving assets for subsequent generations (legacy) and maintaining sufficient reserves for unexpected contingencies that have not been earmarked for other purposes (liquidity). Lifestyle, Longevity, Legacy, and Liquidity are the 4 L's of retirement income.

Changing Risks in Retirement

It is important to understand from the very outset how retirement-income planning must handle different risks than does traditional wealth management. Retirees have less capacity for risk, as they are more vulnerable to a reduced standard of living when risks manifest. Those entering retirement are crossing the threshold into an entirely foreign way of living.

Risks in retirement can be summarized into seven general categories, listed in Exhibit 1.4.

Exhibit 1.4

Retirement Risks

- Reduced earnings capacity
- Visible spending constraint
- Heightened investment risk
- Unknown longevity
- Spending shocks
- Compounding inflation
- Declining cognitive abilities

1. *Reduced earnings capacity.* Retirees face reduced flexibility to earn income in the labor markets as a way to cushion their standard of living from the impact of poor market returns. One important distinction in retirement is that people often experience large reductions in their risk capacity as the value of their human capital declines. As a result, they are left with fewer options for responding to poor portfolio returns.

Risk capacity is the ability to endure a decline in portfolio value without experiencing a substantial decline in your standard of living. Prior to retirement, poor market returns might be counteracted with a small increase in the savings rate, a brief retirement delay, or even a slight increase in risk taking. Once retired, however, people can find it hard to return to the labor force and are more likely to live on fixed budgets.

2. *Visible spending constraint.* At one time, investments were a place for saving and accumulation, but retirees must try to create an income stream from their existing assets—this puts an important constraint on their investment decisions. Taking distributions amplifies investment risks (market volatility, interest-rate volatility, and credit risk) by increasing the importance of the order of investment returns in retirement.

It can be difficult to reduce spending in response to a poor market environment. Portfolio losses could have a more significant impact on standard of living after retirement, necessitating greater care and vigilance in response to portfolio volatility. Even a person with high risk tolerance (the ability to stomach market volatility comfortably) is constrained by his or her risk capacity.

The traditional goal of wealth accumulation is generally to seek the highest returns possible in order to maximize wealth, subject to one's risk tolerance. Taking on more risk before retirement can be justified, because many people have greater risk capacity at that time and can focus more on their risk tolerance.

However, the investing problem fundamentally changes in retirement. Retirees worry less about maximizing risk-adjusted returns and more about ensuring that their assets can support their spending goals for the remainder of their lives. The objective is to sustain a living standard while spending down assets over a finite but unknown length of time. The spending needs that will eventually be financed by the portfolio no longer reside in the distant future.

In this new retirement calculus, methods of balancing trade-offs between upside potential and downside protection can change. Retirees might find that the risks associated with seeking return premiums on risky assets loom larger than before, and they might be prepared to sacrifice more potential upside growth to protect against the downside risks of being unable to meet spending objectives.

The requirement to sustain an income from a portfolio is a new constraint on investing that is not considered by basic wealth-maximization approaches such as portfolio diversification and modern portfolio theory (MPT). In MPT, cash flows are ignored, and the investment horizon is limited to a single, lengthy period. This simplification guides investing theory for wealth accumulation. When spending from a portfolio, the concept of sequence-of-returns risk becomes more relevant as portfolio losses early in retirement increase the percentage of remaining assets withdrawn as income. This can dig a hole from which it becomes increasingly difficult to escape, as portfolio returns must exceed the growing withdrawal percentage to prevent further portfolio depletion. Even if markets subsequently recover, the retirement portfolio cannot fully rebound. The sustainable withdrawal rate from a retirement portfolio can fall below the average return earned by the portfolio during retirement.

3. *Heightened investment risk.* As we just discussed, retirees experience heightened vulnerability to sequence-of-returns risk when they begin spending from their investment portfolios. Poor returns early in retirement can push the sustainable withdrawal rate well below what is implied by long-term average market returns.

The financial-market returns that you experience near your retirement date matter a great deal more than you may realize. Retiring at the beginning of a bear market is incredibly dangerous. The average market return over a thirty-year period could be quite generous, but if negative returns occur as you start spending from your portfolio, withdrawals can deplete wealth rapidly and leave a much smaller principal to benefit from any subsequent market recovery, even with the same average returns over a long period. In other words, what happens in the markets during the fragile decade around the retirement date matters a lot.

The dynamics of sequence risk suggest that a prolonged recessionary environment early in retirement, even without an accompanying economic catastrophe, could jeopardize the retirement prospects for particular groups of retirees. Some could experience much worse retirement outcomes than those retiring a few years earlier or later. It is nearly impossible to see such an instance coming, as devastation for any group of retirees is not necessarily preceded or accompanied by devastation for the overall economy.

4. *Unknown longevity.* The fundamental risk for retirement is unknown longevity. In other words, how long will your retirement plan need to generate income? The length of your retirement could be much shorter or longer than your statistical life expectancy. A long life is wonderful, but it is also costlier and a bigger drain on resources. Half of the population will outlive their statistical life expectancy—which is only increasing with scientific progress. For many retirees, the fear of outliving resources may exceed the fear of death.

5. *Spending shocks.* Unexpected expenses come in many forms, including:

   - Unforeseen need to help family members,
   - Divorce,
   - Changes in tax laws or other public policy,
   - Changing housing needs,
   - Home repairs,
   - Rising health-care and prescription costs, and
   - Long-term care.

   Retirees must preserve flexibility and liquidity to manage unplanned expenses. When attempting to budget over a long retirement period, it is important to include allowances for such contingencies.

6. *Compounding inflation.* Retirees face the risk that inflation will erode the purchasing power of their savings as they progress through retirement. Low inflation may not be noticeable in the short term, but it can have a big impact over a lengthy retirement, leaving retirees vulnerable. Even with just 3 percent average annual inflation, the purchasing power of a dollar will fall by more than half after twenty-five years, doubling the cost of living.

   Sequence-of-returns risk is amplified by greater portfolio volatility, yet many retirees cannot afford to play it too safe. Short-term fixed-income securities might struggle to provide returns that exceed inflation, causing these assets to be quite risky in a different sense: they may not be able to support a retiree's long-term spending goals. Low-volatility assets are generally viewed as less risky, but this may not apply when the objective is to sustain spending over a longtime horizon. Even low levels of inflation can create dramatic impacts on purchasing power over a long period. Retirees must keep an eye on the long-term cumulative impacts of even low inflation and position their assets accordingly.

7. *Declining cognitive abilities.* Finally, a retirement-income plan must incorporate the unfortunate reality that many retirees will experience declining cognitive abilities that hamper portfolio management and other financial decision-making skills. For the afflicted, it will become increasingly difficult to make sound portfolio investments and withdrawal decisions in advanced age.

In addition, many households do not equally share the management of personal finances. When the spouse who manages the finances dies first, the surviving spouse can run into serious problems without a clear plan in place. The surviving spouse can be left vulnerable to financial predators and financial mistakes. Survivors often become more exposed to fraud and theft.

While liquidity and flexibility are important, retirees should also prepare for the reality that cognitive decline will hamper the portfolio management skills of many as they age, increasing the desirability of advanced planning and automation for late-in-life financial goals.

◉ Retirement-Income Tools

Retirement plans can be built to manage varying risks by strategically combining different retirement-income tools. As a result, retirement-income planning is now emerging as a distinct field.

Total-Return Investment Portfolios

Making systematic withdrawals from a well-diversified investment portfolio is a common way to obtain retirement income. However, systematic withdrawals do not protect a retiree from longevity risk or sequence-of-returns risk, and they may only protect from inflation risk when asset returns can keep up with inflation. This approach has its benefits, such as the potential to keep your nest egg growing so you can leave a large inheritance, as well as a sense of technical liquidity that could become true liquidity if markets perform well. On the other hand, a total-returns approach is particularly vulnerable to declining cognitive abilities, as managing distributions and investments requires complex financial decision-making.

Individual Bonds

Leaving behind the purely total-returns perspective, another viable option is to hold fixed-income assets to their maturity to guarantee upcoming retirement expenses. Often, this is done to support short- and/or medium-term spending, with a more aggressive investment portfolio with higher expected returns and growth to be deployed for expenses in the long term.

Holding bonds to their maturity can keep you from selling them at a loss, which may help alleviate sequence-of-returns risk. Individual bonds do not provide longevity protection, however. While they may provide technical liquidity, selling them early to cover contingencies could result in capital losses as well as the loss of assets that were earmarked to cover future spending. Traditional bonds are exposed to inflation risk, but Treasury inflation-protected securities (TIPS) can be used to lock in the purchasing power of money in real terms.

As for the risk of declining cognitive abilities, managing the bond-and-investment portfolio may still be complicated, but bonds can provide additional behavioral benefits. Knowing that income is accounted for over the next several years can help retirees stay the course and not sell off their stock positions in a panic after a market decline. Retirees can take comfort in the knowledge that there will be time for their stocks to recover before they must be sold. By using bonds to provide income for a fixed number of years, it may also be easier for retirees to understand why their overall asset allocation is what it is. Individuals may not be clear on why their portfolios have 60 percent stock funds and 40 percent bond funds, but if they instead think in terms of how building a bond ladder with 40 percent of their assets allows for eight years of income, for instance, then the nature of their asset-allocation choice may be clearer.

Income Annuities, Traditional Pensions, and Other Annuity Types

Partially annuitizing your assets can also provide an effective way to build an income floor for retirement. Income annuities, as opposed to individual bonds, provide longevity protection by hedging the risks associated with not knowing how long you will live. Fixed annuities can be real or nominal, and the initial payments can begin within one year (single-premium immediate annuities or SPIAs) or be deferred to a later age (deferred-income annuities, or DIAs). Some employers still offer traditional defined-benefit pensions, which can also be treated as income annuities.

Whether to annuitize, when to annuitize, how much to annuitize, and whether to build a ladder of annuities over time are all important questions. Annuities protect from longevity and sequence of returns risk, and they can protect from inflation risk if a real annuity is purchased. Because income from them continues automatically, they also provide protection for cognitive decline. David Laibson, a professor at Harvard University, refers to income annuities as "dementia insurance." They help manage many risks. But they provide no growth potential, and life-only versions will not support an inheritance by themselves. In general, they are also not liquid if more funds are needed for unplanned contingencies. However, partial annuitization combined with investments can be an effective way to create true liquidity on the balance sheet.

Income annuities represent only a small percentage of total annuity sales; countless types of annuities can be used for many different purposes. Fixed deferred annuities can act as an alternative to CDs or savings accounts; investment-only deferred variable annuities can provide a source of tax-deferred savings during the accumulation phase; and fixed indexed annuities (a newer name for equity-indexed annuities), immediate variable annuities, and deferred variable annuities with guarantee riders can all provide various combinations of guaranteed income, liquidity, and upside-growth potential. Related nonannuity investment options include income-guarantee riders on an investment portfolio and using financial derivatives on your own to generate the same types of outcomes as some types of annuities.

Social Security

Social Security is the ultimate form of income annuity, and it is generally one of the largest assets on the retirement balance sheet. For a high-earning couple, the present value of lifetime Social Security benefits could exceed one million dollars. Social Security provides protection from inflation, longevity, and sequence-of-returns risk as well as survivor benefits. Retirement benefits can begin as early as age sixty-two, but the benefits grow through age seventy if you wait. If you view the deferred benefits from ages sixty-two to sixty-nine as the premium for buying a larger annuity starting at seventy, delaying Social Security can be like the best annuity money can buy. It offers a better deal than any commercial providers. Because Social Security income continues automatically over time, it also provides protections for cognitive decline. The only risk Social Security does not help manage is a spending shock, as you cannot borrow against your future benefits to obtain greater liquidity today.

Housing Wealth

The other major asset for most households, outside of investment portfolios and Social Security, is home equity, or housing wealth. My colleague Professor Jamie Hopkins is fond of quoting Census Bureau data showing that home equity represents 68 percent of total household assets (not counting Social Security benefits) for married couples in the United States at age sixty-five. This is too large an asset to treat as an afterthought.

Housing wealth can be used in a variety of ways in retirement. If you carefully choose housing that will allow for aging in place, then it can provide inflation protection and some protection against the uncertain costs related to long-term care. With cognitive or long-term care needs, housing could be used to put off institutional living, and then housing wealth could be redeployed to cover the costs of institutional living when it becomes necessary. With a reverse mortgage, home equity can become a liquid buffer asset that reduces exposure to sequence-of-returns risk or to cover unexpected contingencies. I will conclude this chapter with an overview of potential uses for home equity that can be facilitated through a reverse mortgage.

Long-Term Care Planning

One of the largest spending shocks facing a retired household is the cost of ongoing long-term care. A retirement-income plan must account for this, and various tools are available to help control the impacts of long-term care costs on family wealth.

The four main options for meeting long-term care needs include:

- self-funding,
- Medicaid,
- traditional long-term care insurance, and
- new hybrid insurance products that combine long-term care coverage with an annuity or life insurance.

Planning in advance for long-term care needs can help control the impact of spending shocks and cognitive decline.

Other Assets, Insurance, and Income Sources

A hodgepodge of other retirement-income tools can also be a valuable source of support for retirement. Decisions made about Medicare or other health insurance can help mitigate the risks of large health-care spending shocks throughout retirement. Feasible part-time work can help support a more fulfilling lifestyle; bring income to help mitigate risks related to market returns; and maintain an active mind, helping to limit the severity of cognitive difficulties.

Another source of support is social capital: the ability to obtain help from family members, the community, and the social safety net. Access to these opportunities can help mitigate harms related to the various retirement risks. Other potential assets that are less exposed to market risk and may be available to support retirement goals include life insurance, business holdings, and rental income from real estate.

◉ Potential Strategies for a HECM Reverse Mortgage

With this overview of retirement-income planning, it becomes easier to understand the variety of ways that home equity can be fit into a retirement-income plan. The next few chapters discuss important preliminaries. Chapter 2 is about general housing decisions for retirement and important concepts around aging in place. Chapter 3 discusses the background and history of reverse mortgages in the United States. Chapter 4 explains how reverse mortgages work.

Exhibit 1.5

The Spectrum of Reverse-Mortgage Strategies

Spend Down Credit (Favors Low Margin Rate/High Up-Front Costs)

Portfolio/Debt Coordination for Housing (Chapter 5)	• Pay off an Existing Mortgage • Transition from Traditional Mortgage to Reverse Mortgage • Fund Home Renovations to Allow for Aging in Place • HECM for Purchase for New Home
Portfolio Coordination for Retirement Spending (Chapter 6)	• Spend Home Equity First to Leverage Portfolio Upside Potential • Coordinate HECM Spending to Mitigate Sequence Risk • Use Tenure Payments to Reduce Portfolio Withdrawals
Funding Source for Retirement Efficiency Improvements (Chapter 7)	• Tenure Payments as Annuity Alternative • Social Security Delay Bridge • Tax Bracket Management or Pay Taxes for Roth Conversions • Pay Premiums for Existing Long-Term Care Insurance Policy
Preserve Credit as Insurance Policy (Chapter 8)	• Support Retirement Spending After Portfolio Depletion • Protective Hedge for Home Value • Provides Contingency Fund for Spending Shocks (In home care, health expenses, divorce settlement)

Preserve Credit (Favors High Margin Rate/Low Up-Front Costs)

With this general understanding in place, chapters 5 to 8 are heart of the book. Conventional wisdom seems to treat the home as a reserve asset that can be sold to support long-term care needs and otherwise is the source of legacy. These chapters provide quantitative assessments to compare this conventional wisdom against other reverse-mortgage strategies for a view of the overall impact on the retirement-income plan.

These chapters also go into greater depth on the potential ways that a HECM reverse mortgage can be used within a retirement-income plan. Exhibit 1.5 provides a framework for organizing the potential strategies—a roadmap for those four chapters. Strategies are ordered from those that spend available credit more quickly to those that open the line of credit as a type of insurance backstop that may never need to be tapped. These four general reverse-mortgage utilization categories include:

- debt coordination for housing (chapter 5);
- portfolio coordination for retirement spending (chapter 6);
- a resource to fund retirement-income strategy enhancements (chapter 7);
- as 'insurance' for various retirement contingencies (chapter 8).

Finally, chapter 9 closes the book with practical advice about deciding on a reverse mortgage. This includes an assessment of reverse-mortgage risks, along with tips on how to find a lender and other issues to think about.

Further Reading

Pfau, Wade D. 2017. *How Much Can I Spend in Retirement? A Guide to Investment-Based Retirement Income Strategies.* McLean, VA: Retirement Researcher Media. http://amzn.to/2xLgXGC

CHAPTER 2

Housing Decisions in Retirement

● Should I Stay or Should I Go?

Developing a plan to meet housing needs is an important part of a retirement income strategy. A home provides an emotional anchor of daily comfort, shelter, memories, and proximity to both friends and community. It is also a major source of wealth for retirees and near-retirees. For many Americans, home equity provides a substantial part of their net worth, and it is often larger than the value of the household's investment portfolio.

Expenses related to the home (property taxes, utility bills, home maintenance, and upkeep) can add up to a significant portion of the overall household budget. The Center for Retirement Research at Boston College analyzed numbers for retired couples aged sixty-five to seventy-four in 2010 and found that housing expenses represented 30% of the typical household budget.

Joseph Coughlin, the director of the MIT Agelab, created three basic questions to identify quality of life issues for retirement:

- Who will change my light bulbs?
- How will I get an ice cream cone?
- Who will I have lunch with?

An essential part of answering these questions involves solving for the right type and location of housing. These questions illustrate how our lives will change as our bodies slow down and health issues or other aspects of aging make us less mobile. They focus on:

- whether we can continue to live in and properly maintain the same home,
- whether we have access to a community that lets us continue to enjoy basic conveniences even if we may stop driving our own cars, and
- what will happen to our social lives and opportunities to remain active as old friends also become less mobile or move away.

Will we live in communities that keep these key aspects of quality living accessible to us? For new retirees, any difficulty with answering these questions may still reside in the distant future, but the major life changes associated with retirement provide a good opportunity to reflect on the different possibilities and develop a set of contingency plans.

Ultimately, one of the greatest dangers to quality of life in retirement is the risk of becoming increasingly isolated and having only television or web surfing to pass the time. On the emotional side, the housing decision may relate in large part to figuring out how to best answer Coughlin's three questions over the long term.

Because of its important connection to the emotional and financial aspects of retirement, it is worthwhile to think carefully about housing options and potential uses for home equity. As you grow older, the importance of living somewhere with social connections, transportation options, quality health care, and long-term care services increases. In the more immediate present, you need to think about where to live, how long to stay there, and whether to move later in retirement. Plenty of justifications exist for staying put or for moving early in retirement.

First, consider reasons for moving. These relate primarily to the changing emphasis of life's priorities and needs. For instance, empty nesters may no longer require a home large enough to accommodate an entire family. Large homes require more cleaning, maneuvering, heating and cooling, and maintenance. Children may have moved to other parts of the country, and new retirees may wish to be closer to their grandchildren.

While you work and raise children, you are pretty firmly locked in place by proximity to your job and your kids' school. Upon retirement, a move to a community with a less highly rated school and no daily commute could mean lower property taxes and increased savings for your retirement budget. You may save more by moving to a state with a more tax-friendly environment for retirees. This newfound freedom can create a whole new set of options that might not have been realistic in the past. In addition, with more time to focus on hobbies and interests, you could move closer to places that can better fulfill them (e.g., a college town or a warmer climate).

Finally, the aging process will slowly reduce mobility, and you can move with a long-term housing plan in mind, increasing your chances of aging in place and quick access to important medical care.

All that being said, most retirees choose to stay put and it may be more common than we often believe. For instance, Richard Green and Hyojung Lee studied households using the 2006–2010 American Community Survey and found that the propensity to move peaks in an individual's twenties and then declines until about fifty, staying at the lowest relative levels. So, older individuals are less likely to move, and the rate of moving does not rise at typical retirement ages.

Retirees have family, community ties, and friendships that they do not wish to leave behind. Many have significant memories and good feelings about their homes and wish to maintain the stability and familiarity that those represent. A home can be an important part of one's emotional identity, so many choose not to leave that anchor behind.

Homeowners tend to take pride in ownership and might not care to go through the moving process again. New technologies and the possibility of renovating one's home can also make aging in place easier than in the past.

Exhibit 2.1 provides a summary of considerations regarding whether to stay or move in retirement.

Exhibit 2.1

Items to Consider When Deciding to Stay or Move

- Availability of interesting leisure activities
- Diverse transportation options
- Access to quality health care
- Agreeable climate and community
- Access to family and friends
- Ability to maintain social ties
- Ability to age in place in your home
- Housing prices
- Costs of living and affordability of new location
- State income taxes
- State sales tax
- State inheritance tax
- Local property taxes and costs of municipal services
- Other state tax rules regarding retirement-income sources (e.g., Social Security and inheritance tax)

◉ Aging in Place

Aging in place refers to the growing industry around helping members of the aging population remain in their homes despite functional or cognitive impairments. This way, they can maintain familiarity and comfort, and proper planning can help delay any future move to institutional settings. Merrill Lynch and AgeWave conducted a survey of retirees aged fifty and older and found that 85 percent viewed their own home as the preferred location for receiving long-term care. Home care is often the more desirable and less expensive option, and it can be extended with sufficient planning. Government agencies have expressed support for the idea and have promoted the concept, as aging in place often requires less contribution from government programs like Medicaid than do nursing homes or assisted-living facilities.

Exhibit 2.2 provides a list of issues to consider when searching for a home and community that can support aging in place.

Exhibit 2.2

Conditions to Facilitate Aging in Place

Home Characteristics and Renovations (Universal Design Features)

- Walk-in showers and other bathroom safety features such as grab bars
- Single-floor living with no stairs (kitchen, bathing facility, and bedroom are all on one floor), or an elevator allowing access to other floors
- Wheelchair accessibility: ramps to the home, wide doors and hallways that can fit a wheelchair, at least one wheelchair-accessible entrance to the home
- Levers for door handles and faucets rather than a twisting knob
- Good lighting in case sight is diminished
- Accessible cabinets and closets as well as lowered counters to allow for cooking while sitting
- Softened flooring to help cushion any falls, but no rugs or other floor items that could create a tripping hazard
- Accessible electric controls and switches that are not too high off the ground
- New technologies to monitor health status and medicine use

Community Infrastructure

- Trusted support for lawn care, snow removal, and home maintenance
- Overall degree of neighborhood safety
- Availability of someone (family or friend) who can provide occasional checks and help you avoid isolation
- Availability of cleaning and food delivery services (including groceries)
- Availability of transportation options outside of using your own car, such as public transportation, taxis or services like Uber, or volunteer services from non-profit organizations
- Access to a social network and enjoyable social activities
- Access to quality health care and long-term care

Aging in place requires planning, and there are several potential paths. If you stay put, renovating your home can make it livable even if you have physical or cognitive impairments. If you move, you can look for a new home with the necessary renovations already in place and a community where many types of care are readily accessible. This sort of move could be to a detached home, condo, or apartment community specifically designed for fifty-five- or sixty-two-plus living, or to an assisted-living facility (ALF) or continuing-care retirement community (CCRC).

◉ Downsizing Your Home

One method for freeing home equity for other uses is to downsize your home. This doesn't necessarily mean moving to a physically smaller home; it can mean moving to a similar-sized home in a less expensive area.

The arithmetic of converting home equity through downsizing is fairly basic. If you pay off the mortgage on a $300,000 home, sell it, and move into a $200,000 home, you've freed up $100,000 of home equity for other uses.

Another possibility is simply selling your home and renting an apartment. This frees up home equity and provides the flexibility to make more frequent moves before settling down.

When analyzing the decision to rent or buy, you'll need to consider factors such as:

- the loss of build-up in home equity and its subsequent growth (or loss),
- savings on property taxes and other types of home maintenance, and
- the ongoing expense of rent, which adds up significantly over time.

When downsizing, you might consider moving to an active community for adults, which could be less expensive and provide organized activities and social support. These types of communities generally do not provide health care or assisted-living options. Continuing-care retirement communities, though, cover potential long-term care needs, and you can move in earlier, avoiding a big move later in life. There are differences in home ownership with these options, as CCRCs generally provide a right to access housing for life (up through nursing care) rather than tangible equity in a home.

If you are looking to downsize for financial reasons, you may wish to first consider your local government's provisions for property-tax deferral or other possibilities. Other options include renting out a portion of your existing home or opening a reverse mortgage (more on this shortly).

An important caveat about downsizing is that it can be dangerous to assume that it will be part of your retirement-income plan. The same study of retirees conducted by Merrill Lynch and AgeWave also found what they refer to as a "downsize surprise," where many retirees who planned to downsize ended up not wanting to do so once they retired.

The survey—composed of retirees fifty and older—revealed that 37 percent have moved in retirement, another 27 percent have not moved but anticipate moving at some point, and 36 percent of retirees do not anticipate moving in retirement. For those not planning to move, the top reason provided was "I love my home."

The highest-ranking reasons for moving included wanting to be closer to family and reducing home expenses. For those who had moved since retirement, 51 percent moved to a smaller home, 19 percent to a same-sized home, and 30 percent to a larger home. For those who chose to upsize, the most important reason given was to have more space for family members (including grandchildren) to visit. The AgeWave study makes clear that downsizing is not the only moving option for retirees, and it should not be viewed as a given.

Further Reading

Center for Retirement Research at Boston College. 2014. *Using Your House for Income in Retirement.*

Coughlin, Joseph F. 2013. "3 Questions Predict Future Quality of Life." *MarketWatch RetireMentors Series* (April 17).

Green, Richard. 2013. "Who Moves? Not Old People." *Forbes* (July 23).

Merrill Lynch and Age Wave. 2015. "Home in Retirement: More Freedom, New Choices."

CHAPTER 3

Reverse-Mortgage Background and History

If, after considering other housing options, you have decided to remain in an eligible home (or move into one), you may want to consider a Home Equity Conversion Mortgage (HECM – commonly pronounced "heck-um")—more commonly known as a "reverse mortgage"—as a source of retirement spending.

The vast majority of reverse mortgages in the United States are HECM reverse mortgages, which are regulated and insured through the federal government by the Department of Housing and Urban Development (HUD) and the Federal Housing Authority (FHA). Other options outside of the federal program pop up occasionally, like jumbo reverse mortgages for those seeking amounts that exceed federal limits.

The HECM program includes both fixed- and variable-rate loans, though fixed-rate loans only allow proceeds to be taken as an initial lump sum, with no subsequent access to a line of credit. We will not concern ourselves with fixed-rate or non-HECM loans here but focus only on variable-rate HECM options that allow for the line of credit. Two cases where a fixed-rate HECM might be a relevant consideration include when the strategy is to refinance a large existing mortgage or when using the HECM for Purchase program.

In the past, any discussion of reverse mortgages as a retirement-income tool typically focused on real or perceived negatives related to traditionally high costs and potentially inappropriate uses of funds. These conversations often included misguided ideas about the homeowner losing title to the home and hyperbole about the "American Dream" becoming the "American Nightmare." Reverse mortgages have been portrayed as a desperate last resort.

However, developments of the past decade have made reverse mortgages harder to dismiss outright. Especially, since 2013, the federal government has been refining regulations for its HECM program in order to:

- improve the sustainability of the underlying mortgage insurance fund,
- better protect eligible nonborrowing spouses, and
- ensure that borrowers have sufficient financial resources to continue paying their property taxes, homeowner's insurance, and home-maintenance expenses.

The thrust of these changes has been to ensure that reverse mortgages are used responsibly as part of an overall retirement-income strategy rather than to fritter away assets.

On the academic side, several recent research articles have demonstrated how responsible use of a reverse mortgage can enhance an overall retirement-income plan. Importantly, this research incorporates realistic costs for reverse mortgages, both in relation to their initial up-front costs and the ongoing growth of any outstanding loan balance. Quantified benefits are understood to exist only after netting out the costs associated with reverse mortgages.

In short, well-handled reverse mortgages have suffered from the bad press surrounding irresponsible reverse mortgages for too long. Reverse mortgages give responsible retirees the option to create liquidity for an otherwise illiquid asset, which can, in turn, potentially support a more efficient retirement-income strategy (more spending and/or more legacy). Liquidity is created by allowing homeowners to borrow against the value of the home with the flexibility to defer repayment until they have permanently left the home.

The media has been picking up on these developments as of late, and coverage is improving. For instance, Pat Esswein wrote a long follow-up to an April 2016 column about reverse mortgages in the October 2017 issue of *Kiplinger's* named, "Use Your Home to Get More Income."

But the trend of positive coverage is still a new phenomenon, and with so much preexisting bias, it can be hard to view reverse mortgages objectively without a clear understanding of how the benefits exceed the costs. To understand their role, it is worth stepping back to clarify the retirement-income problems we seek to solve (as outlined in chapter 1).

Retirees must support a series of expenses—overall lifestyle spending goals, unexpected contingencies, legacy goals—to enjoy a successful retirement. Suppose that retirees only have two assets—beyond Social Security and any pensions—to meet their spending obligations: an investment portfolio and home equity. The task is to link these assets to spending obligations efficiently while also mitigating retirement risks like longevity, market volatility, and spending surprises that can impact the plan.

The fundamental question is this: How can these two assets work to meet spending goals while simultaneously preserving remaining assets to cover contingencies and support a legacy? Spending from either asset today means less for future spending and legacy. For the portfolio, spending reduces the remaining asset balance and sacrifices subsequent growth on those investments. Likewise, spending a portion of home equity surrenders future legacy through the increase and subsequent growth of the loan balance. Both effects work in the same way, so the question is how to best coordinate the use of these two assets to meet the spending goal and still preserve as much legacy as possible.

When a household has an investment portfolio and home equity, the "default" strategy tends to value spending down investment assets first and preserving home equity as long as possible, with the goal of supporting a legacy through a debt-free home. A reverse mortgage is viewed as an option, but it's only a last resort once the investment portfolio has been depleted and vital spending needs are threatened.

The research of the last few years has generally found this conventional wisdom constraining and counterproductive. Initiating the reverse mortgage earlier and coordinating spending from home equity throughout retirement can help meet spending goals while also providing a larger legacy. That is the nature of retirement-income efficiency: using assets in a way that allows for more spending and/or more legacy.

Legacy wealth is the combined value of any remaining financial assets plus any remaining home equity after repaying the reverse-mortgage loan balance. Money is fungible, and the specific ratio of financial assets and remaining home equity is not important. In the final analysis, only the sum of these two components matters.

For heirs wishing to keep the home, a larger legacy offers an extra bonus of additional financial assets after the loan balance has been repaid. The home is *not* lost.

While taking money from the reverse mortgage reduces the home-equity component, it does not necessarily reduce the overall net worth or legacy value of assets. Wanting to specifically preserve the home may be a psychological constraint, which leads to a less efficient retirement. As Tom Davison of ToolsforRetirementPlanning.com has described the matter to me in our discussions, a reverse mortgage allows a retiree to gift the value of the house rather than the house itself. Should the heir wish to keep the house, the value of the house received as an inheritance can be redeployed for this purpose.

◎ The Underlying Mechanisms of How Reverse Mortgages Can Help

Two benefits give opening a reverse mortgage earlier in retirement the potential to improve retirement efficiencies in spite of loan costs. First, coordinating withdrawals from a reverse mortgage reduces strain on portfolio withdrawals, which helps manage sequence-of-returns risk. Investment volatility is amplified by sequence-of-returns risk and can be more harmful to retirees who are withdrawing from, rather than contributing to, their portfolios. Reverse mortgages sidestep this sequence risk by providing an alternative source of spending after market declines.

The second potential benefit of opening the reverse mortgage early—especially when interest rates are low—is that the principal limit that can be borrowed from will continue to grow throughout retirement. Reverse mortgages are nonrecourse loans, meaning that even if the loan balance is greater than the subsequent home value, the borrower does not have to repay more than the home is worth. Sufficiently long retirements carry a reasonable possibility that the available credit may eventually exceed the value of the home. In these cases, mortgage-insurance premiums paid to the government are used to make sure that the lender does not experience a loss. In addition, the borrower and/or estate will not be on the hook for repaying more than the value of the home when the loan becomes due. This line-of-credit growth is one of the most important and confusing aspects of reverse mortgages. I will return to line-of-credit growth for a deeper explanation later.

As the government continues to strengthen the rules and regulations for reverse mortgages and new research continues to pave the way with an agnostic view of their role, reverse mortgages may become much more common in the coming years. Many Americans rely on home equity and Social Security as their two primary retirement assets.

As Dr. Sandra Timmerman, gerontologist and visiting professor at The American College, said:

> The transition to retirement is a wake-up call for many middle-income Baby Boomers who haven't saved enough money to last a lifetime and want to age in place. With their homes as a major untapped financial resource, the smart use of reverse mortgages will be their saving grace.

◉ Addressing the Bad Reputation of Reverse Mortgages

Before discussing how reverse mortgages can fit into your retirement-income plan, it is worthwhile to first consider in greater detail the bad reputation that reverse mortgages have developed. Some aspects of it are based on misunderstandings; some were once true but have since been mitigated, and some may still remain.

When considering a reverse mortgage, it is important to be responsible with the strategy and not give in to the temptation to treat the reverse mortgage as a windfall and spend it quickly. This point cannot be overemphasized enough, as the natural tendency may be to spend assets as soon as they become liquid. Responsible retirees have little to worry about, but if you lack sufficient self-control, you should handle a reverse mortgage carefully.

Irresponsible borrowers who quickly depleted their assets and suffered later in retirement are part of the reason that reverse mortgages developed

Exhibit 3.1

Addressing the Bad Reputation of Reverse Mortgages

Reasons Reverse Mortgages Have Bad Reputations	Further Discussion

Use Reverse Mortgage Too Quickly for Questionable Expenses

In the past, retirees have opened reverse mortgages to spend the full amount of available credit immediately—perhaps either to overindulge irresponsibly in unnecessary discretionary expenses or to finance shady or even fraudulent investment or insurance products. This jeopardized the role of home equity as a reserve asset for the household.	HUD requires a counseling session and now includes a financial assessment to make sure that sufficient resources will be available to meet homeowner obligations related to keeping a reverse mortgage in place. Set-asides from the line of credit can be carved to ensure payment of future property taxes and other homeowner obligations in the event that sufficient other resources are not available.

Family Misunderstandings

The media has reported on adult children who are surprised to find that they will not inherit the house after their parents passed because their parents used a reverse mortgage.	Such media reports are typically based on misunderstandings on the part of angry children. Articles focus on only one aspect of inheritance (the home) and do not consider how to best meet the retirement spending needs of parents. Children can pay the loan balance and keep the home, and recent research clarifies that strategic use of a reverse mortgage to cover a fixed retirement-spending need is actually more likely to increase the overall amount of legacy wealth available to children at the end. One must also consider whether the parents' assets were best used to meet their own spending goals or to provide a legacy for their children.

Nonborrowing spouses

In the past, younger spouses were taken off a home's title to allow a reverse mortgage to proceed, only to be surprised when the borrower died and the nonborrowing spouse either had to repay the loan or leave the home.	As of 2015, new protections are in place for nonborrowing spouses. They can remain in the home even after the borrowing spouse has passed away. Though nonborrowing spouses cannot continue to borrow funds from the line of credit, they are now able to remain in the home, and lending limits will be based on their age to help protect the insurance fund. In addition, eligible nonborrowing spouses no longer have to worry about loan repayment until they leave the home on their own volition.

Exhibit 3.1

Addressing the Bad Reputation of Reverse Mortgages (continued)

Reasons Reverse Mortgages Have Bad Reputations	Further Discussion
Home Title	
There is a common misconception that the lender receives the title to the home as part of a reverse mortgage.	This enduring myth about the HECM program is simply untrue.
Desperate Borrowers	
Reverse mortgages were taken out by those who were unable to keep up with their property taxes, homeowner's insurance premiums, and home upkeep. This could result in a default that triggered foreclosure.	As of 2015, a financial assessment has been required to ensure that the borrower has the capacity to make these payments. If other resources are not available, set-asides will be carved out of the line of credit to support these payments. These do not become part of the loan balance until they are spent, but they do otherwise limit the amount that you can borrow from the line of credit. Nonetheless, to the extent that the liquidity from the reverse mortgage leads to a behavioral issue of overspending, this is a concern for potential borrowers with limited self-control.
Foreclosure	
Foreclosures for the elderly generated by the inability to meet technical requirements of the loan generated negative media coverage and a misconstruing of the HECM program.	New safeguards have been added, but it is important to keep in mind that such retirements were not sustainable in the first place. Reverse mortgages may still have created net-positive impacts for these households, as their living situations could have otherwise worsened much sooner. For reverse mortgages, monthly repayments are not required, so nonpayment of the loan does not trigger foreclosure. Reverse mortgages may have helped delay what was ultimately inevitable.
High Costs	
Reverse mortgages are expensive to initiate.	In the past, the initial costs for opening reverse mortgages could be as high as 6 percent of the home value. These up-front costs have been reduced dramatically for competitive lenders. Nonetheless, HECM loans originated today include an unavoidable 2 percent up-front mortgage-insurance premium. That adds up to $2,000 per $100,000 of appraised home value. Other closing costs for home appraisal, titling, and other matters similar to traditional mortgages cannot be avoided. That being said, many lenders may charge the full allowed amount for origination charges, while others may reduce origination fees to $0 and even provide credits that partially cover other fees and the insurance premium. Consumers must shop around.

Exhibit 3.1

Addressing the Bad Reputation of Reverse Mortgages (continued)

Reasons Reverse Mortgages Have Bad Reputations	Further Discussion
Taxpayer Risk	
People may worry about taxpayers being on the hook if the mortgage-insurance fund is overburdened by the nonrecourse aspects of these loans.	Reduced housing prices in the 2000s created problems that would be addressed with the Reverse Mortgage Stabilization Act of 2013 to help make sure insurance premiums and lending limits were sufficient to keep the insurance self-sustaining. Further action was taken with rules implemented on October 2, 2017, which increase initial mortgage insurance premiums and reduce initial borrowing amounts and growth rates on the line of credit. These actions have further reduced the risks for the mortgage insurance fund.
Stigma About Using Debt	
Psychologically, some may be challenged by the idea of using a debt instrument in retirement after having spent their careers working to reduce their debt.	This is a psychological constraint. If you think about your investment portfolio and home equity as assets, then meeting spending goals requires spending from assets somewhere on the retiree balance sheet. In this regard, spending from home equity does not necessarily need to be framed as accumulating debt any more than does spending from investment assets. A reverse mortgage creates liquidity for an otherwise illiquid asset. And, though a reverse-mortgage loan balance is a debt, it is different from traditional debt since it does not include an ongoing, fixed repayment obligation. Repayment happens at the end and is limited by the value of the home at that time.

their bad reputation. Recent government changes have been designed to encourage more responsible use, but in many cases, the compensation for loan officers originating these mortgages still may be linked to the initial borrowing amount. As a result, loan officers may suggest taking more out sooner. Consequently, borrowers should seek a loan originator who is not compensated based on the initial lump sum taken from the loan unless they are also working with a trusted financial planner who can help manage this process.

Troubles regarding reverse mortgages are summarized in Exhibit 3.1. Some of them relate to misunderstandings, such as the idea that the lender receives the title to the home, or simple miscommunication among family members about future inheritances.

Other troubles relate to problems that have since been corrected by new HUD regulations. Some of these problems include concerns about withdrawing too much too soon, the potential problems confronting nonborrowing spouses, and foreclosures for desperate borrowers who could not keep up with their property taxes, homeowner's insurance, and home-maintenance requirements.

Other problems have been addressed by the government, though these issues have not necessarily been fully resolved. For many lenders, a notable cost is still involved in initiating a reverse mortgage. As well, though many reforms have been taken to further protect the government's mortgage-insurance fund from claims related to the nonrecourse aspects of reverse mortgages, some individuals may still worry about taxpayer risks related to this matter.

◉ A Brief History of Reverse Mortgages in the United States

Reverse mortgages have a relatively short history in the United States, beginning in a bank in Maine in 1961. The 1987 Housing and Community Development Act saw the federal government systemize reverse mortgages through the Home Equity Conversion Mortgage (HECM) program under the auspices of the US Department of Housing and Urban Development (HUD).

I intend to focus only on HECM reverse mortgages, which are tightly regulated and represent the bulk of reverse mortgages. I will not be discussing programs such as those offered through local governments to provide liquidity for a more limited purpose, or proprietary reverse mortgages, which may appeal to those with homes worth more than the $679,650 FHA lending limit on home values (as of January 1, 2018, and subject to change). (A HECM can be obtained on homes worth more than $679,650, but the funds available through the reverse mortgage will be based on the lesser of the home's appraised value or $679,650.)

In recent years, HUD has frequently updated the administration of the HECM program to address various issues and ensure that reverse mortgages are used responsibly. As a result, descriptions of the program can quickly become outdated, even if they are only a couple of years old. While older materials may explain the concepts adequately, they might be missing key changes. Most recently, important program changes that went into effect on October 2,

2017, mean that anything published before that date do not reflect important characteristics of the program for loan applications made since that date.

Lender standards have tightened, and the number of new reverse mortgages issued has declined after peaking around 110,000 per year in 2008 and 2009. Many borrowers at the peak were financially constrained and unable to keep up with taxes, insurance, and home maintenance. Among those who borrowed, many opted to take out the full available initial credit amount as a lump sum. After spending this down quickly, they were left with no other assets, which led to a number of foreclosures. On top of that, falling home prices meant that many loan balances exceeded the value of the homes being used as collateral when repayment was due, which put greater pressure on the mortgage-insurance fund.

Many older resources on reverse mortgages describe two versions: the HECM Standard and HECM Saver. The HECM Saver was introduced in October 2010 as a contrast to HECM Standard and in response to increased foreclosures. It provided access to a smaller percentage of the home's value, substantially reducing borrowers' mortgage-insurance premiums. It represented a step toward encouraging less up-front use of reverse mortgage credit, but it went largely unused by borrowers.

By September 2013, the Saver and Standard merged back into a single HECM option. The newly merged program provided an initial credit amount that was slightly larger than that of the HECM Saver but substantially less than the HECM Standard. Principal limit factors (more on these in chapter 4) were recalculated to lower available borrowing amounts.

The government also sought to encourage deliberate, conservative use of home equity by implementing penalties and limits. If more than 60 percent of the initial line of credit was spent during the first year, the borrower was charged a higher up-front mortgage-insurance premium on the home's appraised value (2.5 percent instead of 0.5 percent). For a $500,000 home with a $237,500 principal limit, the initial mortgage-insurance premium jumped from $2,500 to $12,500 if more than $142,500 was spent from the line of credit in year one—a $10,000 incentive to lower spending. In addition, borrowing more than 60 percent of the principal limit was only allowed for qualified mandatory expenses like paying down an existing mortgage or using the HECM for Purchase program.

Before September 2013, the HECM Standard mortgage had an initial mortgage-insurance premium of 2 percent of the home value, so the up-front costs for opening a reverse mortgage dropped significantly for those who could stay under the 60 percent limit after HECM Standard and Saver merged. Yet it still paled in comparison to the HECM Saver, as the new 0.5 percent up-front mortgage premium was considerably higher than the previous 0.01 percent value. So, while the new rules were designed to encourage more gradual and deliberate HECM use, the costs for setting up this opportunity relative to the HECM Saver increased.

Two important additional consumer safeguards came into full effect in 2015. The first relates to new protections for nonborrowing spouses who don't meet the minimum age requirement of sixty-two. In the past, when one spouse was too young, the solution was typically to remove that spouse from the house title. This created a problem when the borrowing spouse died first and the loan balance became due. Without sufficient liquidity or the ability to refinance, the nonborrowing spouse could be forced out of the home.

HUD implemented safeguards for nonborrowing spouses in 2014 and further clarified them the following year. As of spring 2015, eligible nonborrowing spouses now have the right to stay in the home after the borrower dies or leaves, as the loan balance no longer needs to be paid until after the nonborrowing spouse has also left the home. In order to do this, the nonborrowing spouse must have been the spouse when the loan was closed, must be named as a nonborrowing spouse, and must continue to occupy the property as a primary residence and maintain the usual taxes, insurance, and home upkeep. These protections apply for loans made after August 2014.

To be clear, while nonborrowing spouses may stay in the home, they are not borrowers. Once the borrower has left the home, there is no further ability to spend from the line of credit, and any term or tenure payments stop. However, interest and mortgage-insurance premiums continue to accrue on any outstanding loan balance. The existing rules contain an important caveat: should the borrower move to an institution such as a nursing home for at least twelve months, the loan may become due even if the nonborrowing spouse remains in the home.

The principal limit factors (PLFs) published on August 4, 2014, accounted for nonborrowing spouses. PLFs are now provided for ages eighteen and older to account for nonborrowing spouses who are significantly younger than the borrower. Before these changes, PLFs were only needed for ages sixty-two and older. The PLF is based on the younger of the borrower and eligible nonborrowing spouse.

Though nonborrowing spouses cannot spend from the reverse mortgage, they may remain in the home for many more years, so initial HECM proceeds must be lowered to protect against loan balances exceeding the home's value. Aside from the expansion to account for nonborrowing spouses, the August 2014 PLFs underwent further downward revisions to limit the initial available credit amount in order to ensure that mortgage-insurance premiums could cover the risk of loan balances exceeding the home's value.

The other new consumer safeguard implemented in 2014 and effective in 2015 is a more detailed financial assessment for potential borrowers to ensure that they have sufficient means to pay property taxes, homeowner's insurance, maintenance and upkeep, and homeowner's-association dues. Determination that a potential borrower will struggle to meet these obligations with assets from outside home equity does not disqualify them from receiving a HECM. Life expectancy set-asides (LESAs) can now be carved out of the line of credit to cover these expenses. Interest on these set-asides does not accrue until the money is spent, but the set-asides prevent borrowers from taking too much from the line of credit and becoming unable to meet the terms required to stay in the home. These new set-asides grow at the effective rate, not the expected rate used for earlier set-asides, a point whose meaning will become clearer after I explain how reverse mortgages work in the next chapter. This was done to clarify earlier confusion created when set-asides grew at a different rate than everything else.

Concerns should be raised about the viability of an overall retirement-income plan when it is necessary to create large set-asides within the line of credit in order to make it work. In some cases, a reverse mortgage might simply be a source of liquidity to cover expenses and allow the borrower to stay in the home while using other limited resources to cover retirement-living expenses.

And this is where the program stood when the first edition of this book went to press in fall 2016. More recently, on August 29, 2017, HUD announced a series of new changes to the HECM program parameters that subsequently went into effect for new HECM applications made after October 2, 2017. In chapter 4, I will explain in full detail what all of these rules and terms mean, but, briefly, the new rules that this book must incorporate since the first edition was published include:

- The initial mortgage-insurance premium when opening a reverse mortgage is now 2 percent of the home value, up to the $679,650 lending limit. This has changed from a previous dual strategy that depended on the amount borrowed in the first year.
- The ongoing mortgage-insurance premium on the loan balance has been reduced to 0.5 percent from the previous 1.25 percent.
- A new table of principal limit factors was issued; these generally result in a reduced initial borrowing amount with the reverse mortgage, at least when interest rates are low.
- The floor on the expected rate used to calculate initial borrowing amounts on a reverse mortgage was reduced from 5.06 percent to 3 percent, which does have some interesting implications in our low-interest-rate environment.

A final recent change issued on September 19, 2017, was to begin allowing nonborrowers to remain on the home title. In the past, only borrowers could remain on the home title. Eligible nonborrowing spouses received protections to be able to stay in the home, but they could not be on the home title. Now they can, as can any other homeowners, such as siblings or children of the borrower. This creates a new category of ineligible nonborrowers that can remain on the home title today. Any homeowners that wish to remain on the home title must also go through the reverse-mortgage counseling session and sign some loan documents as part of the borrower's application process. Since these ineligible nonborrowers do not have protections to stay in the home, their ages are not relevant for determining the initial principal limit. It is still determined based on the youngest of the borrowers or eligible nonborrowing spouses.

Further Reading

Esswein, Patricia Mertz. 2017. "Use Your Home to Get More Income." *Kiplinger's Personal Finance* (October), 38–40.

The US Department of Housing and Urban Development provides details on HECM rules and contact information for housing counselors at www.hud.gov.

CHAPTER 4

How Reverse Mortgages Work

The next step to understanding how reverse mortgages fit into retirement-income planning is to see how they work. Since the program's start in the 1980s, there have been more than one million HECMs initiated in the United States. As mentioned in chapter 3, this discussion is based on the variable-rate HECM, the only option that includes a line of credit. It became popular after 2013. In 2016 and in 2017 through September, the *FHA Single Family Production Report* shows that variable-rate HECMs accounted for 90 percent of the HECMs issued.

(Other reverse-mortgage options include fixed-rate HECMs and proprietary jumbo reverse mortgages that exist outside of the HECM program and are not subject to the rules and guarantees afforded to HECMs. Fixed-rate HECMs could be considered in cases where a large initial-lump sum distribution is desired without a need for an additional line of credit.)

◉ Eligibility Requirements for a HECM Borrower

The basic requirements to become an eligible HECM borrower are:

- age (at least sixty-two);
- equity in your home (any existing mortgage can be refinanced with loan proceeds);
- financial resources to cover tax, insurance, and maintenance expenses;
- no other federal debt;
- competency; and

- receipt of a certificate from an FHA-approved counselor for attending a personal counseling session on home-equity options.

HUD provides a list of approved counselors on its website.

For your *property* to be eligible, it must:

- serve as your primary residence;
- meet FHA property standards and flood requirements;
- be an FHA-eligible property type (this includes single-family homes, two-to-four unit homes with one unit occupied by the borrower, HUD-approved condominium projects, and manufactured homes meeting FHA requirements);
- pass an FHA appraisal; and
- be maintained to meet FHA health and safety standards.

If your home does not meet all standards, some home improvements may also be required for you to initiate a reverse mortgage.

The obligations to pay property taxes, homeowner's insurance, and home maintenance should not be viewed as extraordinary, as they are required for any type of mortgage, not just reverse types. This protects the lender by keeping up the value of the collateral for the loan.

◉ The Initial Principal Limit: Measuring Available Credit

Reverse mortgages use their own jargon, and it is important to understand the meaning of three key terms: (1) principal limit factor (PLF), (2) expected rate, and (3) effective rate. The last two terms sound similar but work in different ways.

The *principal limit* represents the credit capacity available with a HECM reverse mortgage. We need to understand how to calculate the initial principal limit when the reverse mortgage is opened, as well as how the principal limit grows over time. The initial principal limit is calculated with the *expected rate,* while principal limit growth is calculated with the *effective rate.*

PLFs are published by HUD; the current PLF table applies for loans with FHA case numbers assigned on or after October 2, 2017. Because HECMs are nonrecourse loans, the principal limit that can be borrowed must be less than the home's value to reduce the potential for the loan balance outgrowing it. For this reason, factors are updated over time (generally every several years) to manage the risk to the insurance fund.

The basic idea behind reverse mortgages is that the value of the home will eventually be used to repay the loan balance. While the loan balance occasionally ends up exceeding the home's value, the program would be unsustainable if this happened frequently. When the loan balance exceeds the home's appraised value upon the loan becoming due, the insurance fund makes up the difference to protect both the borrower and lender (an important reason that insurance premiums exist).

The available credit amount is determined primarily by:

- the appraised home value;
- the homeowner's age (or, for couples, the age of the younger eligible spouse—and one spouse must be at least sixty-two);
- a lender's margin; and
- the ten-year LIBOR swap rate.

Together, the lender's margin and the swap rate add up to the expected rate.

Expected Rate = 10-year LIBOR swap rate + lender's margin

The PLF determines the borrowing amount as a percentage of the appraised home value, up to the FHA mortgage limit of $679,650. The expected rate is meant to estimate the compounding series of shorter-term interest rates over the next ten years, which provides an estimate for the future path of effective rates. The expected rate is used with the age of the younger spouse to determine the PLF, or the percentage of the home's appraisal value that may be borrowed. If the home's appraisal value exceeds $679,650, this serves as a maximum to which the PLF is applied.

It is important to note that the meaning of the term *age* is a bit more complicated than just equaling your literal age: it is rounded up if your birthday falls within six months of the first day of the month in which the loan is closed. For instance, say that someone is sixty-five years old when his or her loan closes during April. Six months after April 1 is October 1.

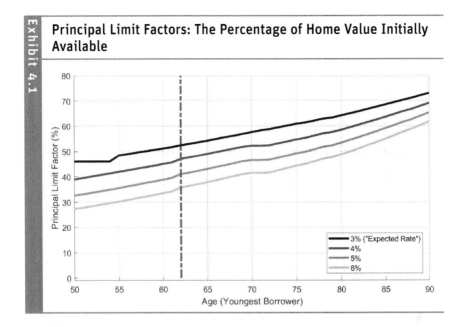

Principal Limit Factors: The Percentage of Home Value Initially Available

Exhibit 4.1

- 3% ("Expected Rate")
- 4%
- 5%
- 6%

Y-axis: Principal Limit Factor (%)
X-axis: Age (Youngest Borrower)

If this person turns sixty-six by the end of September, his or her age is counted as sixty-six for the purposes of determining the PLF. But if the borrower's next birthday is in October or later, the proper age to use for determining the principal limit is sixty-five.

Exhibit 4.1 provides a visual for how these PLFs vary by age and expected rates. Though the range for expected rates is now allowed to vary from 3 percent to 18 percent, the figure shows only for the lower end of the spectrum, because this is what is relevant for our current low-interest-rate environment. The percentage of home value increases when the age of the youngest borrower or nonborrowing spouse is higher and when the expected rate is lower. The PLF is based on a present-value calculation: more can be provided initially when the time horizon is shorter and when the interest rate is lower.

The current low-interest-rate environment provides an advantage when opening a reverse mortgage, as the PLF is higher. Interest rates are quite important relative to age for determining the PLF. For example, with an expected rate of 5 percent, the PLF is 41 percent when the youngest eligible borrower is sixty-two. However, should the rate rise to 6 percent on account of a 1 percent increase in interest rates, the youngest borrower would have

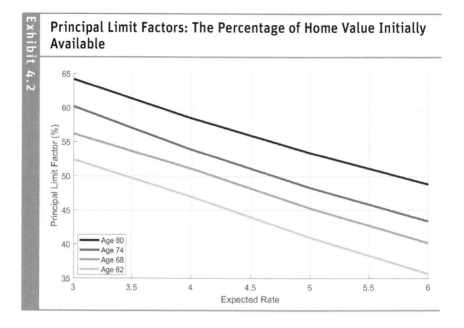

Exhibit 4.2

Principal Limit Factors: The Percentage of Home Value Initially Available

Principal Limit Factor (%)

- Age 80
- Age 74
- Age 68
- Age 62

Expected Rate

to be sixty-nine before the PLF again reaches 41 percent. In this case, it takes seven years for the age impact to offset a 1 percent rise in interest rates.

The October 2017 rules have reduced the importance of interest rates relative to before, as my first-edition example required eighteen years instead of seven before the PLF reached its previous level after a 1 percent increase in interest rates. Nonetheless, the interest-rate effect is still strong.

Because the expected rate is so important for determining initial borrowing amounts, a future increase in interest rates could work to counteract any benefits from an increasing age in determining the PLF for a new reverse-mortgage contract. Exhibit 4.2 provides a similar perspective, but with age and expected rates swapped on the horizontal axis. Again, we observe lower principal-limit factors when expected rates are higher. Increasing ages support higher principal-limit factors across the range of expected rates.

The PLF is the percentage of the home's value initially available. If the principal limit then grows at the "expected rate" thereafter, it is expected to grow to equal the appreciated home value when the loan becomes due (either upon death or leaving the home).

Principal Limit Factor Tables: October 2017 vs. August 2014

The updated HECM rules that went into effect in October 2017 provided a new table of PLF factors to be used for determining initial borrowing amounts from a reverse mortgage. The previous table was in effect since August 2014. The impact of the new factors on borrowing amounts is not uniform across the spectrum of expected rates, though at least for lower interest rates and for younger ages, the initial borrowing amounts have generally declined.

Exhibit 4.3 provides a sampling of PLF factors at different ages and expected rates to see some of these effects. Under the old rules, the expected rate faced a floor of 5 percent (or, to be precise, 5.06 percent). At this expected rate, we can observe notable drops in the PLFs with the updated rules. For instance, at age sixty-two, the PLF decreased from 52.4 percent to 41 percent under the new rules. However, note that at a 7 percent expected rate, the PLF did not change. It was 31.2 percent under the old and the new rules. With a 7 percent expected rate, the PLF even increased slightly at age sixty-six. There is a lack of uniformity with the PLF changes; they were not lowered in all cases.

Exhibit 4.3

A Sampling of Principal Limit Factors pre- and post-October 2017

| | EXPECTED RATE | | | | | | | | | |
| | 3% | | 4% | | 5% | | 6% | | 7% | |
Age	Old	New	Old	New	Old	New	Old	New	Old	New
62	n/a	52.4%	n/a	47.0%	52.4%	41.0%	39.5%	35.7%	31.2%	31.2%
66	n/a	54.9%	n/a	49.7%	54.9%	43.8%	42.1%	38.6%	33.8%	34.1%
70	n/a	57.6%	n/a	52.2%	57.6%	46.5%	45.1%	41.5%	36.5%	37.0%
74	n/a	60.2%	n/a	53.9%	60.6%	48.3%	48.4%	43.4%	40.1%	39.0%
78	n/a	62.9%	n/a	57.1%	64.0%	51.8%	52.0%	47.1%	43.8%	42.8%

For example, with the current table from October 2017, the PLF is 41 percent when the youngest borrower is sixty-two and the expected rate is 5 percent. The government's specific assumptions are not provided publicly, but if we assume a 2 percent growth rate for home appreciation and a remaining life expectancy of thirty-one years to age ninety-three, then we can replicate this actual value for the PLF. A home appreciation rate of 2.57 percent combined with a life expectancy to one hundred (thirty-eight years) also makes the calculation work.

The government might use a different combination of values for these two variables, but the below formula shows the basic idea of how the PLF is calculated:

$$PLF = \left(\frac{1 + \text{home value growth rate}}{1 + \text{expected rate}} \right)^{\text{remaining life expectancy}}$$

◉ Up-front Costs for Opening a Reverse Mortgage

Up-front costs for reverse mortgages come in three categories.

1. Origination fee. First, the mortgage lender can charge an origination fee. Under the HECM program, these fees are currently permitted to be up to 2 percent of the value for homes worth $200,000 or less. The lender may charge up to $2,500 if this calculation leads to a fee lower than that. For homes worth between $200,000 and $400,000, the maximum allowed origination fee is $4,000 plus 1 percent of the home's value above $200,000. For homes worth more than $400,000, the maximum origination fee is $6,000. These fees are the maximum allowed by the government. Lenders have discretion to reduce or waive these fees, and they may even offer credits for other fees. These lenders may either charge higher lender margins to offset the fee reductions, or they earn revenue primarily by originating loans to sell on the secondary market rather than through charging origination fees.

Prior to the October 2017 rules change, I saw cases in which companies offered total up-front costs of $125 for the required counseling session with a $0 origination fee, along with credits to cover the mortgage insurance and other closing costs described in the following paragraphs. With the higher initial mortgage-insurance premium created by the October 2017 rules, it is no longer feasible for lenders to provide credits for these full up-front costs. The $125 deal may become something instead along the lines of a $5,000 deal. Shopping around will continue to be important. Some lenders also offer lower origination fees for borrowers willing to accept a higher lender's margin.

2. Initial mortgage-insurance premium. A second source of up-front costs is the initial mortgage-insurance premium paid to the government, which is based on the value of the home. This fee has changed over time. Since October 2017, it is 2 percent of the home value (up to $679,650). The initial mortgage-insurance premium is $2,000 per $100,000 of home value, up to $13,593 for the $679,650 limit.

The purpose of the mortgage-insurance premium is to cover the guarantees provided by the FHA to the lender and borrower. This protection ensures that the borrower has access to the full principal limit even if the lender goes out of business, and the lender is protected for the nonrecourse

A Heads-Up on Up-Front Costs

When I mention total up-front costs, I mean that these are the full costs paid by the borrower at any point. As I noted, the borrower may pay them with other resources or finance them as part of the initial HECM loan balance. Up-front costs can be less than their full retail value, because lenders do not have to charge the origination fee, and they may provide credits for insurance and other closing costs. Lenders that can securitize the loans for a premium on the secondary market are frequently able to credit some of the costs for the borrower.

I have heard some lenders use a different way to explain up-front costs. They will say that there are no "out of pocket" costs with a reverse mortgage. What they mean is just that the borrower can finance the up-front costs as part of the initial HECM loan balance. Such lenders do not necessarily intend to be tricky about this, but it is tricky in relation to the terminology I have adopted. Up-front costs and out-of-pocket costs can be misinterpreted as the same thing. Up-front costs can still be high; they are just not paid out of pocket at the beginning. When I speak of low up-front costs, I mean that the up-front costs are actually low. I am not talking about financing the costs to keep them low only at the beginning. When speaking with a lender, it is important to understand the distinction between total up-front costs and what are simply initial out-of-pocket costs.

How Reverse-Mortgage Lenders Make Money

Readers may wonder how reverse-mortgage lenders make money, especially in cases where they credit many of the up-front costs for initiating a mortgage. I noted that they sell the loans—in this case, to Ginnie Mae, for more than the value of the money lent. Ginnie Mae securitizes these loans and sells them to investors, who value these securities for providing government-insured, risk-free returns that, unlike traditional forward mortgages, tend not to be repaid early when interest rates decline.

aspect of the loan. If the home value cannot cover the loan balance, the government will make up the difference for the lender. The allows borrowers to receive a greater access to funds and a growing line of credit that would not be possible without the government guarantees.

3. *Closing costs.* Finally, you have closing costs, which are similar to those for any type of mortgage. These include the costs of the FHA-mandated counseling session, a home appraisal, credit checks, and any costs related to titling. If the appraisal shows shortcomings of the home that could impact health or safety, then additional home repairs may be required as part of setting up the reverse mortgage. A 2011 AARP report estimated that typical closing costs range from $2,000 to $3,000. This range is also consistent with the numbers found currently on a calculator created by the National Reverse Mortgage Lenders Association.

The up-front costs could be paid from other resources or financed from the proceeds of the reverse mortgage loan and repaid later with interest. If up-front costs are financed, the net PLF is what remains after subtracting these costs. You should plan to stay in your home long enough to justify payment of any up-front costs.

◉ Ongoing Credit and Costs

The ongoing costs for a reverse mortgage relate to the interest accruing on any outstanding loan balance, as well as any servicing fees. Servicing fees can be up to $35 per month, though they are generally now incorporated into a higher margin rate rather than charged directly to the borrower. Interest on the loan balance grows at the effective rate:

Effective Rate = One-month LIBOR rate + lender's margin + annual mortgage-insurance premium (0.5 percent)

In October 2017, the one-month LIBOR rate was about 1.25 percent, and the ten-year LIBOR swap rate was about 2.25 percent. If we assume a 2.75 percent lender's margin, that gives us an expected rate of 5 percent and an effective rate of 4.5 percent:

Expected Rate = 2.25 percent + 2.75 percent = 5 percent (for initial principal limit)
Effective Rate: = 1.25 percent + 2.75 percent + 0.5 percent = 4. 5 percent (for principal-limit growth)

Once determined through the PLF, the initial line of credit grows automatically at a variable rate equal to the lender's margin, a 0.5 percent mortgage-insurance premium (MIP), and subsequent values of one-month or one-year LIBOR or Treasury rates. These short-term rates are the only variable part for future growth, as the lender's margin and MIP are fixed at the beginning. Though the variable rate can be a one-month or one-year LIBOR or Treasury rate, in subsequent descriptions I will refer to the one-month LIBOR case. The effective rate is adjusted monthly.

Exhibit 4.4 summarizes how the expected rates and effective rates are calculated and when these rates apply.

Reverse Mortgage Interest Rates

Type	Components	Applies to
Expected Rate	10-year LIBOR swap rate + lender's margin	Initial principal limit factor Set-asides for servicing costs in old mortgages
Effective Rate	1-month LIBOR rate + lender's margin + mortgage insurance premium (0.5 percent)	Ongoing principal limit growth rate Loan-balance growth rate Line-of-credit growth rate Post-2014 set-asides for the financially strained

Exhibit 4.4

The lender's margin rate and ongoing mortgage-insurance premium are set contractually at the onset of the loan and cannot change. The margin rate charged on the loan balance is the primary way that the lender—or any buyer on the secondary market—earns revenue, especially lenders who have forgone the origination and servicing fees. Estimates for reasonable margin rates are generally between 1.75 percent and 4.5 percent, with higher numbers typically being associated with lower origination and/or servicing costs.

Meanwhile, the ongoing mortgage-insurance premium helps ensure that the government can meet the obligations for the guarantees it supports through the HECM program to both the lenders and borrowers. I noted that the government guarantees two things: that the borrower will be able to access the fully entitled line of credit regardless of any financial difficulties on the part of the lender, and that the insurance fund will make the lender whole whenever payment falls due and the loan balance exceeds 95 percent of the appraised value of the home. The government fund also bears the risk with the tenure- and term-payment options as distributions are guaranteed to continue when the borrower remains in the home, even if the principal limit has been fully tapped.

The insurance premiums protect homeowners from not having to pay back more than the value of the home in cases where the loan balance exceeds this value. The lender is protected as well, as the FHA pays the difference in such cases. While this could potentially leave taxpayers on the hook if the mortgage-insurance premiums are not sufficient to cover these cases, the government attempts to stay on top of this matter. Mortgage-insurance premiums and principal limit factors have been adjusted over time to help keep the system in balance.

I wrote in the first edition that if the option to open a line of credit and leave it unused for many years grew in popularity, further changes might be needed to keep the mortgage insurance fund sustainable. One intended purpose for the new October 2017 rules was to accomplish this by reducing the likelihood that the principal limit grows larger than the value of the home.

◉ Spending Options for a Variable-Rate HECM

A reverse mortgage can fit into a retirement-income plan in several ways, but it is important to first understand your options for taking distributions from a HECM. Most current HECM reverse mortgages use an adjustable interest rate, which allows the proceeds from the reverse mortgage to be taken out in any of four ways. The substantially less popular fixed-rate HECM, not otherwise discussed in this book, allows only for a one-time, up-front, lump-sum distribution option.

The spending options for a variable-rate HECM include:

1. *Lump-sum payment.* One takes out a large amount initially, though not necessarily the full amount available.

2. *Tenure payment.* Works similarly to an income annuity, with a fixed monthly payment guaranteed to be received as long as the borrower

remains in the home (which, to be clear, is not the same as dying, as the borrower may leave the home while still alive or otherwise fail to meet homeowner obligations). Tenure payments allow for additional spending from the HECM even when the line of credit has been fully used. The mortgage-insurance fund bears the risk that payouts and loan growth from the tenure-payment option exceed the subsequent value of the home when the loan becomes due.

For those interested in the mechanics, the available monthly tenure payment can be calculated using the PMT formula in Excel:

$$=PMT(rate, nper, pv, 0, 1)$$

in which
- *rate* is the expected rate plus the 0.5 percent mortgage-insurance premium, all divided by twelve to convert into a monthly amount. This gives us the rate at which the loan balance is expected to grow. For example, a 5 percent expected rate makes this number 5.5 percent/12 = 0.458 percent;

- *nper* is the number of months between the age of the youngest borrower (or eligible nonborrowing spouse) and age one hundred. For example, a new sixty-two-year-old has 456 months (thirty-eight years) until he or she turns one hundred; and

- *pv* is the net principal limit from the reverse mortgage. It is found by multiplying the principal limit factor by the appraised value of the home (up to $679,650) less any up-front costs financed with the loan and any set-asides. For instance, a sixty-two-year-old with a $500,000 home and a 41 percent principal limit who pays up-front costs from other resources will have a $205,000 net principal limit.

And so, PMT (5.5 percent/12, 456, 205000, 0, 1) = $1,068 for a monthly tenure payment. Annually, this adds up to $12,816 from the reverse mortgage.

My reverse-mortgage calculator at https://www.retirementresearcher. com/reverse-mortgage-calculator also provides these calculations for tenure payments.

3. *Term payment.* This is a fixed monthly payment received for a fixed amount of time. Calculating a term payment is similar to calculating a tenure payment. The only difference is that nper is smaller, as it is the desired number of months that the term payment should last. If the number of months pushed the term past age one hundred, a tenure payment would be used instead. As with a tenure payment, the full amount of term payments will be paid even if rising rates cause the loan balance plus new payments to exceed the principal limit.

   As an example, consider an eight-year term payment, which could be used as part of a strategy to delay Social Security. The monthly term payment would be PMT (5.5 percent/12, 8*12, 205000, 0, 1) = $2,632, or $31,588 annually.

4. *Line of credit.* Home equity does not need to be spent initially—or ever. A number of strategies involve opening a line of credit and then leaving it to grow at a variable interest rate as an available asset to cover a variety of contingencies later in retirement. Distributions can be taken from the remaining line of credit whenever desired until the line of credit has been used in its entirety.

Some of these spending options can be combined.

Using a portion of the line of credit to create tenure (or term) payments and leaving the remainder to grow is called "modified tenure" (or "modified term"). You can also change spending options over time, in which case updated term or tenure payments would be based on the available line of credit. Should tenure or term payments begin at a later date, the expected rate used to calculate the initial principal limit would remain the same throughout the term of the loan.

◉ Understanding Why and How the HECM Line of Credit Grows

A mortgage's effective rate is applied not just to the loan balance but also to the overall principal limit, which grows throughout the duration of the loan. How the effective rate is applied may sound technical, but it is an overwhelmingly important point to understand in order to grasp the value of opening a line of credit.

Typically speaking, the principal limit, loan balance, and remaining line of credit all grow at the same rate. In rare cases in the past, a reverse mortgage included a servicing set-aside that grew at a high-enough expected rate that the set-aside balance grew even as expenses were paid. A consistent growth rate is the case for all new loans today, since any new set-asides will also grow at the same effective rate.

The sum of the loan balance, line of credit, and any set-aside is the principal limit. Interest and insurance premiums are charged on the loan balance, not on set-asides or the line of credit. Set-asides are not part of the loan balance until they are actually used, but they limit access to the line of credit. Though interest and insurance premiums are not levied on set-asides or the line of credit, both components grow as *if* interest and premiums were charged.

When funds are borrowed, the line of credit decreases and the loan balance increases. Conversely, voluntary repayments increase the amount of the line of credit, which will then continue to grow at the effective rate, allowing for access to more credit later.

The following equation shows this relationship, which always holds for recent reverse mortgages because all variables in the equation grow at the same effective rate:

Principal Limit = loan balance + available line of credit + set-asides

Exhibit 4.5 expresses the same concept. The overall principal limit consists of the loan balance, remaining line of credit, and any set-asides. Again, all these factors grow at the same effective rate, which increases the size of the overall pie over time. If no further spending or repayment happens over time, the proportions of each of these components of the principal limit remain the same since they all grow at the same rate. Having unused line of credit grow is a valuable consideration for opening a reverse mortgage sooner rather than later. It is also a detail that creates a great deal of confusion for those first learning about reverse mortgages, perhaps because it seems that this feature is almost too good to be true.

I believe that the motivation for the government's design of the HECM reverse-mortgage program is based on an underlying assumption that

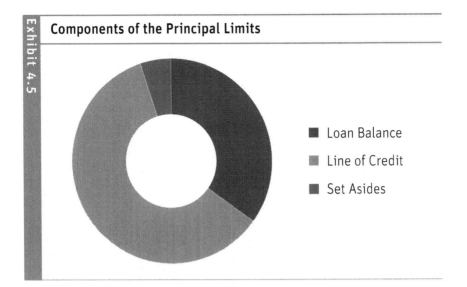

Exhibit 4.5

Components of the Principal Limits

- ■ Loan Balance
- ■ Line of Credit
- ■ Set Asides

borrowers will spend from their line of credit sooner rather than later. Implicitly, the growth in the principal limit would then reflect growth of the loan balance more than the growth of the line of credit. In other words, designers assumed that the loan balance would be a large percentage of the principal limit.

The line of credit happens to grow at the same rate as the loan balance, and, if left unused, it can grow quite large. There was probably never an expectation that such open lines of credit would just be left alone for long periods. However, as I will discuss, the bulk of the research on this matter since 2012 suggests that this sort of delayed gradual use of the line of credit can be extremely helpful in prolonging the longevity of an investment portfolio.

A simple example may help illuminate the concept further. Consider two individuals. Each opens a reverse mortgage with a principal limit of $100,000. For simplicity's sake, we'll assume that ten years later, the principal limit for both borrowers has grown to $200,000.

Person A takes out the entire $100,000 initially from the reverse mortgage (100 percent of the principal limit is the loan balance). For this person, the $200,000 principal limit after ten years reflects a $200,000 loan balance (the loan balance is still 100 percent of the principal limit), which consists of the initial $100,000 received plus another $100,000 divided between accumulated interest payments and insurance premiums.

Person B takes a different route and opens a reverse mortgage but does not use any of the credit, so the $200,000 principal limit at the end of ten years reflects the value fully of the line of credit. The principal limit was still 100 percent in the line of credit. This value was calculated with an implicit assumption that interest and insurance payments have been accruing, even though they haven't.

Person B can then take out the full $200,000 after ten years and have the same loan balance as Person A, but Person B has received $200,000 rather than $100,000. At this point, Person B has bypassed the accumulation of interest and insurance to the detriment of the lender and the mortgage-insurance fund. Person B has really benefited from this action; it has been called the "ruthless option" by some academics who study reverse mortgages.

◉ Why Open a Reverse Mortgage Before It Is Actually Needed?

Another question that will arise: Would the line of credit ultimately be larger if opened earlier rather than later? We can further explore this question with a more realistic example. Exhibit 4.6 below provides an illustration of the impact of opening a reverse mortgage at different points in time using a few basic assumptions.

Still keeping matters relatively simple, I assume that the one-month LIBOR rate stays permanently at 1.25 percent and the ten-year LIBOR swap rate remains permanently at 2.25 percent. The lender's margin is assumed to be 2.75 percent, and home inflation is 2 percent.

For a sixty-two-year-old with a home worth $250,000 today, the exhibit charts three values over time until the individual is ninety. The home value grows by 2 percent annually, and it is worth $435,256 by age ninety. The principal limit for a reverse mortgage opened at sixty-two is $102,500 (based on a principal limit factor of 41 percent for the 5 percent expected rate. The principal limit grows at an effective rate of 4.5 percent, and the principal limit is worth $351,544 by age ninety.

Finally, Exhibit 4.6 also shows the available principal limit if the reverse mortgage is not opened until each subsequent age rather than at age sixty-two. By delaying the start of the reverse mortgage, and assuming that the expected rate of 5 percent remains, the principal limit grows because the principal limit factor is higher at advanced ages, and because this factor is applied to a higher home value.

Nonetheless, even at age ninety, the available principal limit for a new reverse mortgage is only $284,222, which is based on a PLF of 65.3 percent applied to a current home value of $435,256. The message from this example is that opening the line of credit earlier allows for greater availability of future credit relative to waiting until later in retirement.

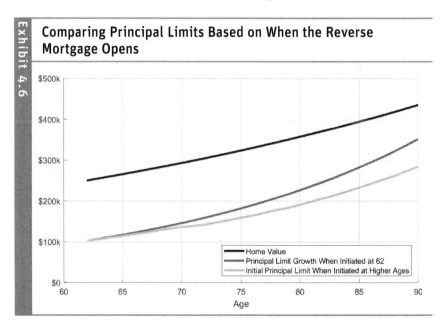

Exhibit 4.6

Comparing Principal Limits Based on When the Reverse Mortgage Opens

Admittedly, Exhibit 4.6 does look less impressive in terms of the potential value of opening the reverse mortgage early compared to the same exhibit from the first edition, before the October 2017 rule changes. Exhibit 4.7 compares the growth in the principal limit for loans from before and after the October 2, 2017, change in program parameters. Under the old rules explained in this book's previous edition, the principal limit could grow more rapidly, as it started from a higher initial base and included an ongoing mortgage insurance-premium of 1.25 percent in the effective rate instead of the current 0.5 percent. By age eighty-three, the principal

Exhibit 4.7

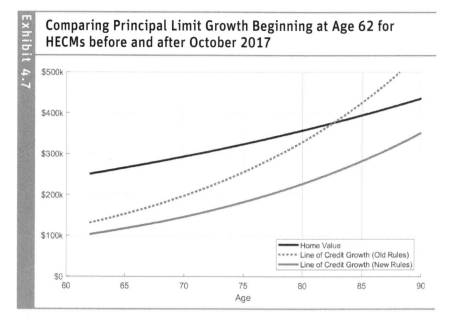

Comparing Principal Limit Growth Beginning at Age 62 for HECMs before and after October 2017

limit exceeded the value of the home—twenty-one years after the loan was initiated. More broadly, Exhibit 4.7 shows how the pace of principal limit growth was substantially slowed by the October 2017 rule change.

This example assumes that interest rates remain low. But if interest rates increase in the future, the value of opening the line of credit today would be greater. Rising future interest rates would help to bring back some of the excitement about line-of-credit growth that was tempered by the October 2017 rule updates. With lower rates today, the available PLF is higher. Then, higher future interest rates would cause the future effective rate to be higher so that the principal limit grows more quickly. Rising rates would also increase the expected rate used to calculate principal limits on new reverse mortgages in the future. This would reduce the principal limit on newly issued future loans. An example of this is provided in Exhibit 4.8. The scenario is the same as in Exhibit 4.6, except that later in the first year of analysis, interest rates permanently increase by 1 percent, which raises the effective rate to 6 percent for HECMs issued at later ages and the effective rate for principal limit growth to 5.5 percent. The exhibit shows the widening gap in available principal limit created by opening the reverse mortgage sooner. If interest rates rise in the future, the case for opening the reverse mortgage sooner than it is potentially needed becomes stronger.

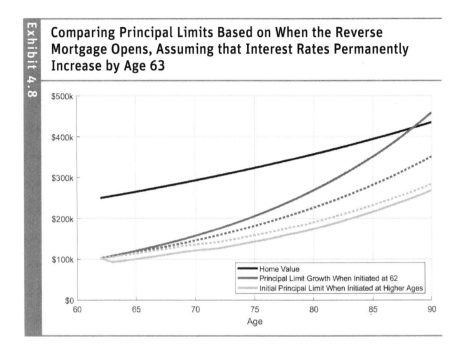

Exhibit 4.8

Comparing Principal Limits Based on When the Reverse Mortgage Opens, Assuming that Interest Rates Permanently Increase by Age 63

Legend:
- Home Value
- Principal Limit Growth When Initiated at 62
- Initial Principal Limit When Initiated at Higher Ages

Y-axis: $0, $100k, $200k, $300k, $400k, $500k
X-axis (Age): 60, 65, 70, 75, 80, 85, 90

All of this may sound too good to be true—and it probably is, to some extent. Perhaps this is why it is difficult to grasp the concept of line-of-credit growth throughout retirement. I've already noted that unused lines of credit work for borrowers to the detriment of lenders and the government's insurance fund. Such use of a reverse mortgage still exists today and would be contractually protected for those who initiate reverse mortgages under the current rules. I wrote in the first edition that at some point in the future, I expect to see new limitations on line-of-credit growth, especially as more people start to follow the findings of recent research on this matter. A round of such limitations came into effect in October 2017 and have weakened the case for the growing line of credit, though value still exists for these strategies.

Line-of-credit growth may be viewed a bit like an unintended loophole that has been strengthened by our low-interest-rate environment. Further limitations on line-of-credit growth could potentially be created someday for newly issued loans. Until then, research points to this growth as a valuable way that reverse mortgages can contribute to a retirement-income plan, as I will describe in later chapters.

◉ Reverse-Mortgage Calculator

At https://www.retirementresearcher.com/reverse-mortgage-calculator, I have created a calculator that allows users to get a sense of the principal limit available with a HECM reverse mortgage on their homes using the most popular one-month variable-rate option. A preview of the calculator is shown in Exhibit 4.9. The net principal limit is calculated on seven inputs; the amount of cash flow that could be received as a tenure payment for those seeking this option is also provided. An optional eighth input also allows a term-payment amount to be calculated.

The first input is the *Home's Appraised Value.* This value is then compared with the $679,650 FHA lending limit to determine the *HECM eligible amount* (the eligible amount is the lesser of the two).

The next two inputs are the current *10-year LIBOR Swap Rate* and the *Lender's Margin,* which together compose the expected rate. The ten-year swap rate is automatically updated, and so it is not necessary for users to change this value—but the calculator provides flexibility to adjust it if desired.

The next input is the *Age of Youngest Eligible (Borrower or Non-Borrower) Spouse.* The four inputs thus far are used to calculate the *Principal Limit Factor.*

Next, inputs for *Loan Origination Fee and Other Closing Costs* are combined with the predetermined cost for the *Initial Mortgage Insurance* premium to determine the total up-front loan cost.

The next input asks for the *Percentage of Up-front Costs to be Financed* by the loan. This would be 0 percent if costs are financed from other resources, 100 percent if fully financed by the loan, or any number in between. The final input is the amount of *Debt Repayment, Repairs, or Other Life-Expectancy Set-Aside Requirements (LESA)* that have been determined as part of the new financial assessments for borrowers. This information about costs and set-asides is then applied to the eligible home value and the PLF to calculate the net available HECM credit with the loan.

Finally, the calculator provides the net amounts available as either tenure or term payments. The tenure payment is calculated assuming a planning

Exhibit 4.9

HECM Calculator: Net Available Line of Credit or Tenure Payment

Home's Appraised Value	$500,000	
HECM Eligible Amount	$500,000	
10-Year LIBOR Swap Rate	2.25%	
Lender's Margin	2.25%	Expected Rate
Monthly Insurance Premium	0.50%	
"Age of Youngest Borrower (or Eligible Non-Borrower Spouse)	65	

		Age	Modified Expected Rate
Principal Limit Factor	45.90%	65	4.500%
Loan origination fee	$6,000	$6,000	<- Maximum Allowed
Initial mortgage insurance	$10,000		
Other closing costs (appraisal, titling, etc.)	$2,500		
Total Upfront Costs	$18,500		
Percentage of Upfront Costs to be Financed	100%		
Debt Repayment, Repairs, or Other Life-Expectancy Set-Aside (LESA) Requirements	$0		
Net Available HECM Credit	**$211,000**		

	Monthly	Annual Rate	Payout
Net Available as a Tenure Payment	**$1,060**	**$12,726**	**5.54%**

Term Payment Calculator

Desired Term Horizon (Years)	8	

	Monthly	Annual
Net Available as a Term Payment	**$2,660**	**$31,922**

horizon of age one hundred and the expected rate plus the ongoing mortgage-insurance premium. The term payment is calculated for a fixed term, though if the desired number of years for the term payment should extend beyond age one hundred, the term payment is automatically adjusted to be the higher value of the tenure payment. Tenure and term payments are both provided as monthly and annual values, and the tenure payment is also represented as a payout rate based on a percentage of the net principal limit plus the financed up-front costs. This payout rate may be helpful as a way to compare with income annuities (see chapter 7).

◉ Deciding on a Package of Costs for a HECM Reverse Mortgage

The discussion of reverse-mortgage costs has several moving parts. Which type of cost combination to choose depends on how you plan to use the line of credit during retirement. Let me reveal the punch line for the following discussion: Those seeking to spend the credit quickly will benefit more from a cost package with higher up-front costs and a lower lender's margin rate. Meanwhile, those seeking to open a line of credit that may go unused for many years could find better opportunities with a package of costs that trades lower up-front costs for a higher lender's margin rate. These options must be considered carefully, and potential borrowers should ask lenders to provide a range of options to consider around different variations for up-front costs and lender's margins.

To summarize the cost discussion, costs determined by the lender include:

- Origination fees
- Other closing costs
- Servicing fees
- Margin rate

Along with the up-front mortgage-insurance premium, which the lender does not control (though some lenders may provide a credit to cover it), the up-front costs include the origination fees and other typical closing costs. The maximum that can be charged for origination fees is set by the government and relates to the home's value, as described before. Lenders have discretion to charge less than this amount. Smaller lenders with smaller marketing budgets may compete more on price, which can include a lower origination fee, or even credits to offset other fees.

For other closing costs, these fees vary and relate to the typical costs for opening a mortgage (e.g., titling and appraisal charges) as well as payment for the mandatory counseling session. Some lenders may also provide credits to cover some of these costs as well. The only exception is that lenders are not allowed to pay for the counseling session. As for servicing fees, lenders are allowed to charge up to $35 per month, but recently, it is common not to charge an explicit servicing fee and instead include such fees as part of the lender's margin rate.

The final cost to consider is the lender's margin rate. This is not an up-front cost but an ongoing cost charged on the outstanding loan balance. The choice of lender's margin is important because it affects both the initial PLF and the subsequent growth rate of the principal limit. A higher lender's margin reduces the initial principal limit as part of the expected rate, but this principal limit subsequently grows faster, as the margin is also part of the effective rate that determines principal limit growth.

Again, the lender's margin is part of the expected rate, and a higher lender's margin implies a higher expected rate, which in turn implies a lower principal limit factor. For example, if the ten-year LIBOR swap rate is 2.25 percent, a sixty-two-year-old with a $250,000 home could see his initial principal limit fall from $102,500 to $89,250 by choosing a 3.75 percent lender's margin instead of 2.75 percent. This represents a reduction in the principal limit factor from 41 percent to 35.7 percent.

But, the lender's margin is also included as a variable to determine the effective rate—the rate at which the principal limit grows. Remember that the effective rate defines the rate of growth for *both* the outstanding loan balance and the remaining line of credit. Those with a small loan balance benefit from a high lender's margin because it allows their line of credit to grow more quickly, while those with a large loan balance—everything else being the same—prefer a lower lender's margin so that the loan balance does not grow as quickly.

These four ingredients can be combined into different packages by the lender. The best choice depends on how the reverse mortgage is used. When funds will be extracted earlier, it may be worthwhile to pay higher up-front fees coupled with a lower margin rate. However, for a standby line of credit that may go untapped, it could be beneficial to lean toward a higher margin rate combined with a package for reduced origination and servicing fees. Again, some lenders may even offer credits to cover a portion of the up-front fees.

Exhibit 4.10 provides an example of these dynamics for a case of a sixty-two-year-old borrower facing a ten-year LIBOR swap rate of 2.25 percent and a one-month LIBOR rate that stays at 1.25 percent. The exhibit shows the initial principal limits and principal limit growth for three different lender's margins: 1.75 percent, 2.75 percent, and 3.75 percent. For this example, age seventy-seven serves as the crossover point for all three cases. Prior to that age, the principal limit is the largest with the lower 1.75 percent margin, but after age seventy-seven, the principal limit is the largest with the higher 3.75 percent margin.

Note that this example implicitly assumes the same up-front costs for all three scenarios. The crossover age at which the net principal limit becomes larger would be sooner for the high-margin case if it is also accompanied by a package of lender credits to lower the up-front costs.

⊙ Repayment of the HECM Loan Balance

Repayment of a HECM loan balance may be deferred until the last borrower or eligible nonborrowing spouse no longer meets the terms for

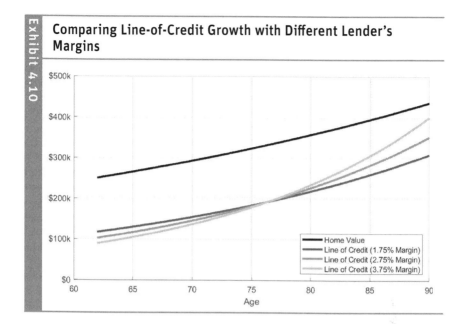

Comparing Line-of-Credit Growth with Different Lender's Margins

Exhibit 4.10

maintaining the loan, either through death, moving or selling the home, or failing to maintain the homeowner's obligations such as paying property taxes. Prior to that time, repayments can be made voluntarily at any point, with no penalty for early repayment, to help reduce future interest due and allow for a larger line of credit to grow for subsequent use.

Again, the HECM is a nonrecourse loan. The borrower (or borrower's estate) is not obligated to pay the lender more than the smaller of the loan balance or 95 percent of the home's appraised value at that time. When the final repayment is due, the title for the home remains with the borrower or estate. Should beneficiaries wish to keep the home, the smaller of the loan balance or 95 percent of the appraised home value can be repaid with other funds. Heirs can also refinance the home with a traditional mortgage should they wish to keep it. If they qualify, heirs might also consider a new HECM to cover the existing loan balance. If they decide to sell the home, they keep anything beyond the outstanding loan balance. Should the loan balance exceed what the home can reasonably be sold for, heirs can simply give the home to the lender through a deed in lieu of foreclosure without worrying about selling it themselves. However, they may be sacrificing a large interest deduction on their taxes if they do this; they should consult a tax professional first.

A deed in lieu of foreclosure is sufficient to extinguish the debt on the reverse mortgage; mortgage insurance from the government will compensate the lender for the difference. Generally, the borrower or heirs have up to 360 days to sell the home or refinance when the loan comes due, but this requires a few extensions from the lender. If you intend to use the full 360 days, it is essential that you maintain regular contact and provide updates to the lender during that time.

◉ Tax Issues

Distributions from reverse mortgages are treated as loan advances and do not reflect taxable income. They are not included in adjusted gross income and do not impact Medicare premiums or the taxation of Social Security benefits. In this regard, proceeds from a reverse mortgage behave the same way as Roth IRA distributions. They can provide a way to increase spending power without pushing you into a higher tax bracket.

A more complex area relates to eligible deductions for reverse mortgages. These taxation issues for reverse mortgages can be complex and are still relatively untested and not fully addressed in the tax code. Researchers Barry Sacks and Tom Davison have recently been exploring deeper into the tax code to better understand these aspects (see Further Reading below). Individual cases vary, so always consult a tax professional with reverse-mortgage experience.

Interest charges, mortgage-insurance premiums, and possibly real-estate taxes may be accumulated as part of the loan balance and may not be repaid until many years later. These are all potentially deductible at different points in time, either as they are incurred or when repaid. After the 2016 tax year, mortgage-insurance premiums are no longer deductible.

Davison has spent a good deal of time exploring IRS publications about these issues, which he has written up at his *Tools for Retirement Planning* blog. He notes that interest can generally not be deducted on taxes until it is actually repaid. Interest payments include interest charged on the borrowed amount and interest compounded on past interest charged. These two aspects of interest may be treated differently for taxes, as interest on interest is not addressed in tax rules.

Repayments on the loan balance are first applied to mortgage-insurance premiums, then servicing fees, interest, and principal amounts borrowed.

So, repayment cannot lead to interest deductions until the MIP and servicing-fee components have been fully repaid. Interest due on the loan balance can potentially be large, so this is an important aspect of tax planning to make sure that repayment timing allows for the best use of this deduction.

Mortgage-insurance premiums can be tax deductible if the borrowing reflects acquisition debt. This is a reverse mortgage use for buying, building, or substantially improving a home. The HECM for Purchase program, as well as major home-improvement projects, should qualify under this criterion. Refinancing acquisition debt with a reverse mortgage also counts for this purpose, such as when a reverse mortgage is used to refinance a traditional mortgage that was used to purchase the home. As of 2018 (for the 2017 tax year), interest deductions are no longer allowed for home equity loan debt taken for purposes other than acquisitions.

Finally, in cases when real-estate taxes are paid from the line of credit, perhaps with a life-expectancy set-aside requirement, any deduction for these taxes should happen as they are incurred rather than repaid.

◉ HELOC vs. HECM

Either a traditional home-equity line of credit (HELOC—pronounced "he-lock") or a HECM can serve as a sources for contingency funds in retirement, but they cannot be combined on a given home. People often think that they should just use a HELOC and not bother with a HECM, but there are important differences between the two options. These must be considered before you take either.

With a HELOC, repayments are required sooner. Users of a HECM can voluntarily repay sooner but are under no obligation to make any repayment before leaving the home.

In addition, retirees may not qualify for a HELOC if they do not have regular income. Though HECMs added new safeguards in 2015 to make sure that they are not used solely as a last resort by those who have otherwise depleted their resources, the qualification requirements are less stringent than for a HELOC. A HECM may still be available with set-asides included to cover tax, insurance, and maintenance obligations. In addition, initial start-up costs may differ for the two options.

A HECM also differs from a HELOC in that its line of credit cannot be canceled, frozen, or reduced. This was a large problem with HELOCs during the 2008 financial crisis. With a HECM, borrowers are protected from lenders modifying their obligations to lend remaining funds in the line of credit. No such protections are available with HELOCs. And, the principal limit for a HECM will grow throughout retirement, unlike the fixed amount available with a HELOC.

In contrast to a HELOC, the HECM is noncancelable, the borrower controls if and when it is used, it has flexible payback control, and the line of credit grows over time independent of home value. If your goal is to set up a liquid contingency fund, make sure that you examine the number of important differences between HECMs and HELOCs.

Further Reading

Davison, Tom, and Keith Turner. 2015. "The Reverse Mortgage: A Strategic Lifetime Planning Resource." *Journal of Retirement 3* (2): 61–79.

Davison, Tom. 2016. "Tax Deductions and Reverse Mortgages." *Tools for Retirement Planning* blog.

Giordano, Shelley. 2015. *What's the Deal With Reverse Mortgages?* Pennington, NJ: People Tested Media. http://amzn.to/2cMwO6Z

Sacks, Barry H., Nicholas Miningas, Stephen R. Sacks, and Francis Vitagliano. 2016. "Recovering a Lost Deduction." *Journal of Taxation* 124 (4): 157–169.

US Department of Housing and Urban Development. 2017. FHA *Single Family Production Report*.

CHAPTER 5

Portfolio Coordination for Retirement Housing

Coordinating housing-related issues with the investment portfolio and a reverse mortgage can be a critical step in a structurally sound retirement plan. Briefly, for those not carrying a substantial mortgage into retirement, a simple HECM use is to fund home renovations to better support the ability to age in place. This may help retirees to remain in their homes for longer, reducing pressure to make (or delaying) a move to a more institutionalized setting. As mentioned in chapter 2, home renovations made with a reverse mortgage could include adding a walk-in bathing facility on the first floor of the home or creating a ramp entrance to the home.

The current chapter focuses on issues related to carrying a traditional mortgage into retirement, or using the HECM for Purchase program to purchase a new home in retirement.

For retirees still carrying a traditional mortgage, two options we will consider are to use a HECM to refinance the existing mortgage and then not worry about repaying the loan balance until it becomes due, or to use the HECM to refinance an existing mortgage and then continue making voluntary payments to reduce the size of the loan balance and increase the available line of credit throughout retirement. These strategies will be tested against options to either pay off the mortgage at the start of retirement with financial assets or to continue making payments on the traditional mortgage in retirement from the financial portfolio until the mortgage debt is extinguished. The important question is whether the ability to mitigate sequence-of-returns risk by refinancing the mortgage with a HECM is beneficial enough to offset the HECM's costs.

In a presentation made at the Financial Planning Association's annual conference in October 2017 about Reverse Mortgage Funding's client base, Tim Jackson indicated that 68 percent of the reverse mortgages that it initiated through financial planners were to refinance existing mortgages carried into retirement. As for the remainder, 20 percent opened a reverse mortgage to set up a growing line of credit, 11 percent used the tenure-payment option for the HECM, and 1 percent used the HECM for Purchase program.

A second matter to consider is how to use the HECM for Purchase program to purchase a new home in retirement. We will compare funding part of a new home's cost with a HECM for Purchase against alternatives such as paying cash for the home or obtaining a fifteen-year traditional mortgage. Again, the question becomes whether the benefits created through the HECM by reducing demands on the portfolio to pay for the retirement home are valuable enough to offset the HECM's costs.

Let's look at some case studies.

◉ Strategies for Carrying a Mortgage into Retirement

More Americans are now entering retirement while still carrying a mortgage. In 2014, the Consumer Finance Protection Bureau reported that the percentage of Americans aged sixty-five and older with a mortgage rose from 22 percent in 2001 to 30 percent in 2011—a rise from 3.8 million to 6.1 million. Among individuals over seventy-five, those who still had mortgages rose from 8.4 percent to 21.2 percent.

Mortgage debt in retirement presents an additional planning challenge. For retirement distributions, fixed payments related to paying off debt create a strain for retirees due to the heightened withdrawal needs triggering greater exposure to sequence-of-returns risk. Exposure rises because the debt payments are fixed and require greater distributions than otherwise, so if there is a market decline early in retirement, the portfolio is further strained as an even greater percentage of what is left in the portfolio must be taken to meet these fixed expenses. Sequence risk is further exacerbated by having a higher distribution need in early retirement on account of the mortgage payments.

The general idea is that a reverse mortgage used primarily to refinance an existing mortgage creates more flexibility for distribution needs from the investment portfolio by removing a fixed expense from household budgeting in the pivotal early-retirement years. During preretirement, it is common to pay off the mortgage more slowly in hopes that investment returns will outpace the borrowing costs on the mortgage. This approach becomes riskier in retirement, as distribution needs heighten the retiree's vulnerability and exposure to market volatility. In addition, a changing tax situation with the loss of wages and the dwindling mortgage balance in retirement could mean losing potential tax deductions for mortgage interest that were taken prior to retirement.

By refinancing the existing mortgage with a reverse mortgage, one could voluntarily continue making the same monthly payments on the loan balance of the reverse mortgage to reduce it and increase the growing credit-line amount for future use. Unlike with a traditional mortgage, these voluntary repayments can be stopped without triggering foreclosure. Voluntary payments can be made strategically when markets are performing well and then stopped when it is necessary to sell assets at a loss to make payments.

The benefit of replacing a mortgage with a reverse mortgage, then, is the reduced exposure to sequence risk. However, it is also important to note that the growth rate on the reverse-mortgage loan balance can exceed the interest rate on the preexisting mortgage, especially if interest rates rise from their current levels. One must balance the trade-offs between the increased flexibility and reduced cash flows to be supported earlier in retirement against the possibility that the final legacy value for assets could be hurt if the HECM loan balance is not repaid for many years. Whether the final legacy increases or decreases when using a reverse mortgage in this way also depends on the performance of the investment portfolio, which may benefit from greater potential growth due to lower distribution needs, leaving more financial assets with more time in the market.

We can analyze these complexities using my standard Monte Carlo simulations, which allow interest rates to start at their lower, current levels but gradually fluctuate toward their historical averages over time. For a retiree carrying a traditional mortgage into retirement, the question becomes what to do with it.

Let's consider six options for those reaching retirement with a traditional mortgage still in place:

1. Use a HECM to refinance the mortgage balance and use the remaining line of credit last to cover retirement spending if the investment portfolio is depleted. Make voluntary payments equal to those of the traditional mortgage in years after portfolio gains to reduce the loan balance and shift more of the principal limit into the line of credit for potential subsequent use.

2. Use a HECM to refinance the mortgage balance and use the remaining line of credit last to cover retirement spending if the portfolio is depleted. Do not make any voluntary payments to reduce the loan balance.

3. Pay off the mortgage at retirement with financial assets; open a HECM as a last resort—only if portfolio assets are depleted later in retirement.

4. Keep the mortgage into retirement, making the required ongoing payments until the mortgage has been fully paid off; open a HECM as a last resort—only if portfolio assets are depleted later in retirement.

5. Keep the mortgage into retirement, making the required ongoing payments until the mortgage has been fully paid off; open the HECM line of credit after the mortgage is paid off and use it last.

6. Pay off the mortgage at retirement with financial assets; open the HECM line of credit and use it last.

These possibilities can provide a sense of how keeping a mortgage compares with using a HECM to refinance it.

Let's look at a case study of a sixty-five-year-old couple entering retirement. Twenty years ago, the couple purchased a $300,000 home with a 20 percent down payment, using a 7.5 percent fixed thirty-year mortgage for the rest of the home price. Then, five years ago, they refinanced their mortgage to take advantage of lower interest rates. Their new mortgage was for fifteen years and had a 3.5 percent fixed rate. At retirement, they have ten years remaining on this mortgage, with annual payments of

$15,574 and a remaining loan balance of $129,526. Over the past twenty years, their home has appreciated at an average rate of 3 percent. It is worth $541,833 today.

They consider a HECM when the ten-year LIBOR swap rate is 2.25 percent, and with a lender's margin of 2.25 percent. For a sixty-five-year old, this translates into an initial PLF of 45.9 percent, with the expected rate of 4.5 percent. Up-front costs include a $6,000 origination fee, an initial mortgage-insurance premium of 2 percent of the home value, plus another $2,500 for other closing costs. These costs total $19,337—and it should be clear that this represents the full retail price in order to avoid biasing the results in favor of the reverse mortgage.

For this scenario, with some shopping around, potential borrowers should be able to get the origination fee waived and perhaps even receive credits for a portion of the other costs. But here, I've assumed that the up-front costs are financed within the loan, leaving a net initial principal limit of $229,365 before refinancing the mortgage (541,833 x 0.459 – 19,337). In cases where the reverse mortgage is opened later, I assume that the maximum eligible home value (currently $679,650) and the closing costs rise with inflation.

Retirement-date financial assets consist of $1 million in a tax-deferred retirement account, and the marginal tax rate is 25 percent. The investment portfolio uses a fifty-fifty asset allocation for stocks and bonds. Finally, the spending goal for retirement expenses, net of any taxes or required mortgage payments, is an inflation-adjusted $40,000. Taxes on portfolio distributions and mortgage payments are added to this spending goal.

Exhibit 5.1 shows the relative results of the first four strategies for meeting the spending goal throughout retirement. The worst outcomes happen either by paying off the mortgage with portfolio distributions at the start of retirement, or carrying the traditional mortgage into retirement and then using a HECM only as a last-resort option after portfolio depletion. These strategies create the most sequence risk, since portfolio distributions are higher to cover mortgage payments as well, leading to a larger negative impact on the retirement plan after a market decline early in retirement. Moving on to higher success rates, the next better strategy is to refinance the existing mortgage into a HECM and use the remaining line of credit as a source of spending if the portfolio depletes later in retirement. After paying the mortgage balance of $129,526, the remaining initial line of credit is $99,839. (My reverse-mortgage calculator can do these calculations.)

Refinancing the mortgage with a HECM noticeably improves success rates relative to strategies that continue with payments from the portfolio. The best outcome is with strategy number (1).

Exhibit 5.1

Probability of Success for a 4 percent Post-Tax Initial Withdrawal Rate, $1 Million Portfolio, $541,833 Home Value, 25 percent Marginal Tax Rate

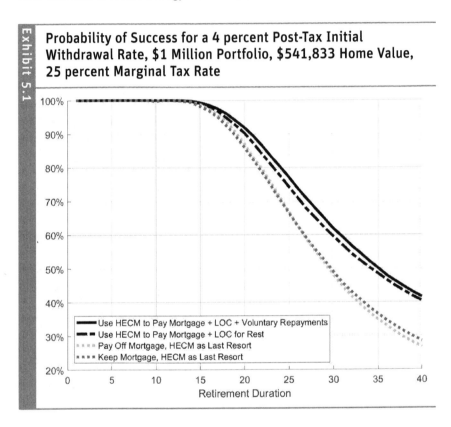

Exhibit 5.2 adds in strategies 5 and 6, which both perform similarly to the best strategy from Exhibit 5.1. Strategy 5 is to keep the mortgage but open a line of credit in ten years after the mortgage is repaid—for later use if the portfolio becomes depleted. Strategy 6 is to pay off the mortgage with a large portfolio distribution at the start of retirement but to immediately open a HECM line of credit and allow it to grow for use later in retirement if the portfolio is depleted.

Exhibit 5.2

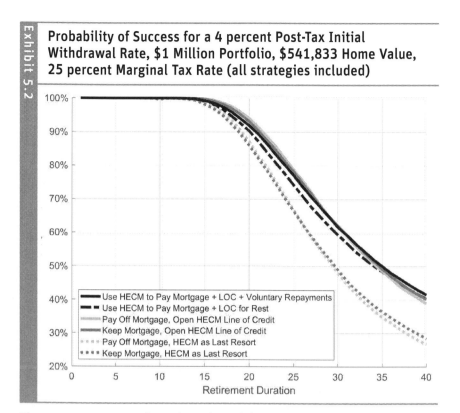

Probability of Success for a 4 percent Post-Tax Initial Withdrawal Rate, $1 Million Portfolio, $541,833 Home Value, 25 percent Marginal Tax Rate (all strategies included)

Legend:
- Use HECM to Pay Mortgage + LOC + Voluntary Repayments
- Use HECM to Pay Mortgage + LOC for Rest
- Pay Off Mortgage, Open HECM Line of Credit
- Keep Mortgage, Open HECM Line of Credit
- Pay Off Mortgage, HECM as Last Resort
- Keep Mortgage, HECM as Last Resort

x-axis: Retirement Duration

These two strategies show the value of the growing line of credit and the difficulty in beating it with other approaches that add to the loan balance more quickly. Refinancing the mortgage with a HECM and then making voluntary repayments is competitive with these two other strategies, indicating that either approach could serve retirees well in improving their odds for success, relative to other strategies that keep a traditional mortgage and use the HECM only as a last-resort option.

However, retirees may be interested in more than just the probability of financing retirement itself successfully. Legacy wealth, or the value of legacy assets available to heirs, can be an important criterion as well. This is defined as any remaining portfolio assets plus any remaining home equity after the reverse-mortgage loan balance has been repaid. If spendable assets are depleted (the portfolio and the entire line of credit) such that the full spending goal cannot be met, legacy values are counted as negative by summing the total spending shortfalls that would manifest either as reduced spending or as a need to rely on one's heirs for additional support (this is a form of "reverse legacy").

Adding the consideration of a negative legacy makes results more meaningful, because it clarifies the magnitude to which a spending goal cannot be achieved. Legacy values are shown on an after-tax basis, assuming that the same 25 percent marginal tax rate applies to portfolio assets—though the possibility of any tax deductions upon repaying the loan balance are not shown.

Exhibit 5.3 shows the legacy value of assets at the median outcome. This means that in 50 percent of cases, legacy values will be less than shown, and in the other 50 percent, values will be greater. The median reflects an average or typical outcome. We can observe very little difference in median legacy values among the six strategies. At least, refinancing the mortgage with a HECM and then making voluntary repayments does provide a slight edge for most retirement durations. The two HECM refinancing strategies also become temporarily flat when the legacy value becomes $0. This results from the HECM still being able to support retirement spending, even though there is no offset to legacy because the loan value has exceeded the value of the home. This triggers the nonrecourse aspects of

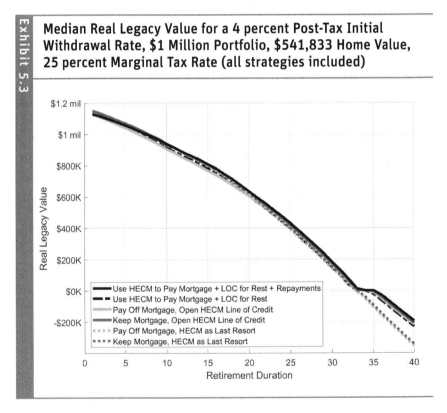

Exhibit 5.3

Median Real Legacy Value for a 4 percent Post-Tax Initial Withdrawal Rate, $1 Million Portfolio, $541,833 Home Value, 25 percent Marginal Tax Rate (all strategies included)

the loan. Once the line of credit fully depletes, then shortfalls begin for all strategies. In these cases, the spending goal was too aggressive and cannot continue to be met after about thirty-one to thirty-three years in the median outcome.

An unlucky outcome is represented by the tenth percentile for legacy wealth. Portfolio returns are poor, and the financial portfolio is quickly depleted. I have not included an exhibit to show this case, because it looks quite similar to the median case. All strategies quickly deplete assets, and there is very little difference to be seen. Strategies do not have a chance to temporarily keep legacy flat at zero, because the portfolio depletes more quickly and the line of credit does not have an opportunity to grow larger than the value of the home before it is spent.

However, there are noticeable differences at the ninetieth percentile for legacy values, as shown in Exhibit 5.4. For these outcomes, the investment portfolio performs well, and distributions can continue without depleting the portfolio. The portfolio is able to grow at a faster rate than the

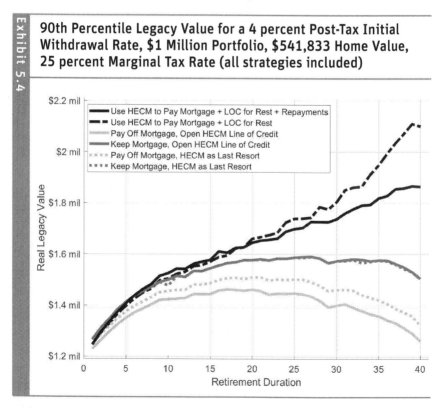

Exhibit 5.4

90th Percentile Legacy Value for a 4 percent Post-Tax Initial Withdrawal Rate, $1 Million Portfolio, $541,833 Home Value, 25 percent Marginal Tax Rate (all strategies included)

Legend:
- Use HECM to Pay Mortgage + LOC for Rest + Repayments
- Use HECM to Pay Mortgage + LOC for Rest
- Pay Off Mortgage, Open HECM Line of Credit
- Keep Mortgage, Open HECM Line of Credit
- Pay Off Mortgage, HECM as Last Resort
- Keep Mortgage, HECM as Last Resort

Y-axis: Real Legacy Value ($1.2 mil to $2.2 mil)
X-axis: Retirement Duration (0 to 40)

principal limit, and so, retirees are able to benefit by keeping more assets in their investment portfolio and spending from the HECM more quickly. The higher subsequent portfolio value more than offsets the growing loan balance for the HECM. The two strategies that refinance into the HECM support the highest legacy values, followed by the two strategies that keep the traditional mortgage into retirement, and, finally, the two strategies that pay off the mortgage with investment assets at the start of retirement.

◉ HECM for Purchase

The HECM for Purchase program began in 2009 as a way to use a reverse mortgage to purchase a new home. The government saw enough people using a costlier and more complicated two-step process—obtaining a traditional mortgage to purchase the home and then using a reverse mortgage to pay off the first one—that it sought to simplify the process and costs. The HECM for Purchase program allows fewer distribution needs from the investment portfolio, because a greater portion of the home's cost can be financed by the reverse mortgage, which does not require payments until the loan balance becomes due.

The HECM for Purchase program can be used to either downsize or upsize a retirement home. For those downsizing, the HECM for Purchase could free up more assets from the sale of the previous home to be used for other purposes. For those upsizing with the financial resources to manage this sustainably and *responsibly*, the HECM for Purchase could allow for a more expensive home—especially considering the possibility that obtaining a traditional mortgage may become increasingly difficult after retirement.

Should the borrower live in the home long enough, the loan balance may grow to exceed the value of the home, setting its nonrecourse aspect into motion. In this situation, one could interpret the HECM for Purchase program as a way to provide housing services as long as the borrower remains eligible for a total cost equal to the portion of the home value and up-front costs not covered by the HECM. Should the borrower leave the home while the loan balance is still less than the home value, the home could be sold with any remaining equity still available to the borrower after the loan is repaid.

In terms of coordinating the use of debt for housing, not having to make a monthly mortgage payment reduces the household's fixed costs and provides potential relief of any need to spend down investments. The HECM for Purchase option can be analyzed relative to paying outright for the home with other assets or opening a fifteen-year mortgage if still feasible.

As a case study on the HECM for Purchase program, consider a sixty-five-year-old couple entering retirement with $1.4 million in a tax-deferred, qualified retirement plan and a desire to purchase a new home costing $300,000. The couple considers whether to fully pay for the home with portfolio distributions, whether to take out a traditional mortgage on the home, or whether to fund a portion of the home's cost with a HECM for Purchase. Again, it is important to note that the traditional-mortgage option may not always be available, as it can be more difficult to qualify for a mortgage when one is no longer working for an income.

Paying cash for the home requires a $300,000 distribution from the investment account plus an additional distribution of $100,000 to cover taxes on the portfolio distributions at a 25 percent marginal tax rate.

For the traditional mortgage, the couple considers a fifteen-year mortgage with a 3.5 percent fixed rate and a 20 percent down payment. This requires $60,000 up-front (plus $20,000 more to cover taxes) and mortgage payments of $20,838 per year for the next fifteen years.

For the HECM for Purchase, the current ten-year swap rate is 2.25 percent, and the lender's margin is 2.25 percent. At age sixty-five, this supports a principal limit factor of 45.9 percent. Full retail up-front costs include $5,000 for the origination fee, $6,000 for the mortgage-insurance premium, and $2,500 for other closing costs for a total of $13,500. The HECM for Purchase covers $137,700, while the investment portfolio covers the other $162,300 for the home and $13,500 for the up-front costs (plus another $58,600 to cover taxes on the distributions).

Exhibit 5.5 includes these six strategies:

1. Use HECM for Purchase to cover as much of the home cost as allowed, and pay cash for the remainder. There is no additional line of credit available with this strategy.

2. Use HECM for Purchase to cover as much of the home cost as allowed, and pay cash for the remainder. But subsequently, for years when

markets provided positive returns, make a voluntary repayment equal to the traditional mortgage payment, but skip these payments after down-market years. Use this built-up line of credit to cover the retirement-spending goal if the investment portfolio depletes.

3. Open a 3.5 percent fixed-rate, fifteen-year conventional mortgage with 20 percent down; open the HECM only as a last resort (if the investment portfolio depletes).

4. Pay cash for the home; open the HECM only as last resort (if the investment portfolio depletes).

5. Open a 3.5 percent fixed-rate, fifteen-year conventional mortgage with 20 percent down. Open a HECM line of credit for later use once the fifteen-year mortgage has been fully repaid.

6. Pay cash for the home and (immediately) open a HECM line of credit on the home to use for retirement spending if/when the investment portfolio depletes.

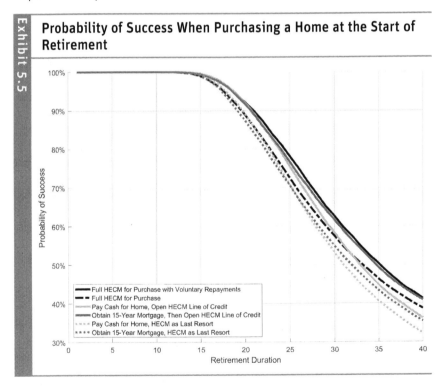

Exhibit 5.5

Probability of Success When Purchasing a Home at the Start of Retirement

Exhibit 5.5 provides the results in terms of the ongoing probability of success in meeting the spending goal throughout retirement. The strategy supporting the highest success rates is number (2)—using the HECM for Purchase and making voluntary repayments on the loan balance. This helps to reduce the need for portfolio distributions early on and provides a mechanism to replenish the credit line for subsequent use.

Strategy (5), with the fifteen-year traditional mortgage followed by opening the HECM line of credit once the mortgage is repaid, has similar outcomes. This strategy also works to take advantage of both reducing initial portfolio distributions and supporting line-of-credit growth for later use. It is a viable strategy as long as the retiree is able to obtain the fifteen-year mortgage.

The next strategies are to pay cash for the home and open the HECM right away or to use the HECM for Purchase but decline to make voluntary repayments such that there will be no line of credit available. Again, the worst-performing strategies both involve using a HECM only as a last-resort option after portfolio depletion and using greater portfolio distributions to pay for the home either immediately or with a fifteen-year mortgage.

As for the legacy value of assets, the outcomes are very similar to those we discussed before, so I do not include exhibits to describe them. At the median, the HECM for Purchase with voluntary repayments is able to support the highest legacy values, but the other strategies are close behind. At the tenth percentile (poor investment returns), outcomes are almost indistinguishable. And at the ninetieth percentile (excellent investment returns), strategies that keep as much as possible in the investment portfolio (such as the HECM for Purchase or the fifteen-year mortgage) support substantially higher legacy outcomes.

Further Reading

Consumer Finance Protection Bureau. 2014. *Snapshot of Older Consumers and Mortgage Debt.*

CHAPTER 6

Portfolio Coordination for Retirement Spending

Maintaining higher fixed costs in retirement increases exposure to sequence risk by requiring a higher withdrawal rate from assets. Drawing from a reverse mortgage has the potential to mitigate this aspect of sequence risk for an investment portfolio by reducing the need for portfolio withdrawals either generally, or just at inopportune times. Coordinating potential spending with distributions from a reverse-mortgage line of credit can potentially be an effective way to help manage the sequence-of-returns risk in retirement.

A HECM line of credit provides a tool for mitigating the impacts of sequence-of-returns risk. Since 2012, a series of research articles has highlighted how the strategic use of a reverse mortgage can either preserve greater overall legacy wealth for a given spending goal, or otherwise sustain a higher spending amount for longer in retirement.

The conventional wisdom on how to treat housing wealth in retirement was to preserve it as a last-resort asset for when all else has failed. The failure to coordinate home equity with the investment portfolio or to attach a growing line of credit to home equity leads to less efficient retirement outcomes.

◉ Foundational Research on Coordinated Spending

Starting in 2012, a series of articles published in the Journal of *Financial Planning* investigated how obtaining a HECM reverse mortgage early in retirement and then strategically spending from the available credit can help improve the sustainability of retirement-income strategies.

We can think of legacy wealth at death as the combined value of any remaining financial assets plus the remaining home equity once the reverse mortgage loan balance has been repaid:

Legacy Wealth = Remaining Financial Assets + [Home Equity – minimum (Loan Balance, 95 percent of Appraised Home Value)]

If we do not worry about the percentage breakdown between these two categories, research reveals the possibility of sustaining a spending goal while also leaving a larger legacy at death. Strategically using home equity can lead to a more efficient strategy than the less flexible option of viewing the home as the legacy asset that must not be touched until everything else is gone. This analysis provides a way to test whether the costs of the reverse mortgage—in terms of the up-front costs and compounding growth of the loan balance—are outweighed by the benefits of mitigating sequence risk. Strategic use of a reverse-mortgage line of credit is shown to improve retirement sustainability, despite the costs, without adversely impacting legacy wealth.

Based on his personal research going as far back as 2004, Barry Sacks got the ball rolling and received widespread recognition for ideas presented in a research article he published with his brother Stephen in the February 2012 issue of the *Journal of Financial Planning*. Barry Sacks is to supplementing retirement spending with a reverse-mortgage line of credit as William Bengen is to the 4 percent rule. He was thinking over a decade ago about how people could use housing wealth as a type of volatility buffer to help mitigate sequence-of-returns risk.

The aptly named article these brothers wrote—"Reversing the Conventional Wisdom: Using Home Equity to Supplement Retirement Income"—set out to present the reverse-mortgage option as something more than a last resort.

The title states their objective clearly. They investigated sustainable withdrawal rates from an investment portfolio coupled with home equity to determine whether asset depletion takes place in any of three different strategies for incorporating home equity into the retirement-income plan:

1. Use a reverse mortgage as a last resort to continue spending only after the investment portfolio is depleted (i.e., the conventional wisdom).

2. Open a reverse-mortgage line of credit at the start of retirement and spend it down first, then transition to using portfolio withdrawals for the remainder of retirement.

3. Open a reverse-mortgage line of credit at the start of retirement and draw from it during any years that follow a negative return for the investment portfolio. This is their "coordinated strategy."

They reversed the conventional wisdom by using Monte Carlo simulations to quantify how spending strategies (2) and (3) enjoyed a higher probability for success and could be sustained for longer than (1).

They also found that the remaining net worth of the household (the value of the remaining financial portfolio plus any remaining home equity) after thirty years of retirement is twice as likely to be larger with an alternative strategy than with the conventional wisdom of saving home equity to be used last.

For withdrawal-rate goals between 4.5 percent and 7 percent of the initial retirement-date portfolio balance, the residual net worth after thirty years was 67 percent to 75 percent more likely to be higher with a coordinated strategy than with a strategy using the reverse mortgage as a last resort. In other words, spending home equity did not ruin the possibility for leaving an inheritance. Instead, the opposite was true.

How is this the case? Essentially, scenarios (2) and (3) provide a cushion against the dreaded sequence-of-returns risk that is such a fundamental challenge to building a sustainable retirement plan. When home equity is used last, retirees are spending down their volatile investment portfolio earlier in retirement and are more exposed to locking in portfolio losses, more easily leading them on the path to depletion.

With option (2), if home equity is spent first, the financial portfolio is left alone in the interim, providing a better chance to grow so that by the time home equity is spent, retirees will be able to continue a given spending amount in their retirement using what is likely be a lower withdrawal rate from a now-larger portfolio. They quantify that the costs and interest paid on the reverse mortgage, while substantial, are less than the benefits the strategy provides to retirees and their beneficiaries.

And option (3) provides a more sophisticated technique to grapple with sequence-of-returns risk by only spending from the reverse-mortgage line of credit when the retiree is vulnerable to locking in portfolio losses: spend from the line of credit only after years in which the financial portfolio has declined.

Sacks and Sacks make clear that their point is not that all retirees should take a reverse mortgage, but that retirees who wish to remain in their homes for as long as possible should view it as more than a last-resort option. If retirees decide to spend at a higher level, which could lead to portfolio depletion and then possibly require them to also generate cash flows from their home equity, there is indeed a better way to approach this task.

In a sign that the time had finally come for the idea of coordinated spending from a reverse mortgage, Harold Evensky, Shaun Pfeiffer, and John Salter of Texas Tech University followed suit with two articles—beginning with the August 2012 issue of the *Journal of Financial Planning*—also investigating the role of a standby line of credit. They developed conclusions quite similar to the Sacks brothers' without knowing of their work.

Harold Evensky said that the motivation for their research came about when the home-equity line of credit (HELOC) he had established as a source of liquidity for his clients kept getting canceled during the financial crisis in 2008. The reverse-mortgage line of credit was guaranteed to be there even in times of market stress. They write, "Although reverse mortgages aren't for everyone, the reluctance to consider use of reverse mortgages in the distribution phase limits the flexibility of distribution strategies."

Their first article in 2012 investigated the use of a HECM Saver line of credit (which, you may recall, had lower costs but was later merged with the HECM Standard in September 2013) as a ready source of cash to be used as a risk-management tool for retirement distributions. The purpose of their research was in line with that of Sacks and Sacks: to test portfolio sustainability using Monte Carlo simulations when portfolio distributions are coordinated with a reverse mortgage.

With a similar objective in mind, they developed a coordinated strategy to better approximate using the reverse mortgage when the portfolio was in jeopardy. Rather than drawing from the reverse-mortgage standby line of credit after years of market downturns, they instead drew from the line of credit whenever the remaining portfolio balance fell below the value indicated by a separate wealth glide-path calculation. They determined the amount of remaining wealth required for each year of retirement to keep the spending plan on a sustainable path through the desired planning horizon. After experimenting with this critical path for remaining wealth, they determined that drawing from the reverse mortgage worked best when remaining wealth fell to less than 80 percent of the wealth-glide path. This helped avoid overuse of the line of credit while still providing a mechanism to avoid selling financial assets at overly depreciated prices, thereby helping mitigate the sequence-of-returns risk.

Another difference between this research and that of the Sacks brothers is that whenever remaining wealth grew enough to be back above the 80 percent barrier for their critical-path trajectory, Evensky and company worked to preserve a larger line of credit for future use by paying back any outstanding balance on the line of credit throughout retirement. This contrasted with Sacks and Sacks, who made no voluntary repayment during retirement.

Evensky has heralded the value of using cash reserves to mitigate sequence risk since the 1980s. Cash provides a drag on potential portfolio returns, but its presence serves as an alternative choice to finance spending and avoid selling other assets at a loss. He suggested having two years of spending in a separate bucket and investing remaining funds with a total-returns investment perspective. He viewed this as a compromise between the offsetting factors of the drag on returns created by holding more cash and not completely protecting the remaining portfolio if market declines last longer than two years.

The reverse-mortgage research of these two articles follows along the same path with the line of credit used in place of a larger cash reserve. In the 2012 article, they replaced the two-year cash reserve with a six-month cash reserve, and they used the line of credit to refill the reserve when necessary in order to reduce the cash drag and provide a source of funds not impacted by declining market returns, which allows funding to last substantially longer than two years.

Their glide-path approach to choosing when to tap the line of credit establishes decision rules that keep better track of cumulative outcomes, so it makes intuitive sense. Their 2012 research uses the line of credit as a source of funds only when the portfolio is below the mark set by the glide path and the cash-reserve bucket has been depleted.

As with Sacks and Sacks, they found that using the standby line of credit improved portfolio survival without creating an adverse impact on median remaining wealth (including remaining home equity). This provided independent confirmation that the reverse mortgage line of credit can help mitigate sequence-of-returns risk without impacting legacy goals. They also confirmed that having a larger line of credit (either through a higher PLF with lower interest rates or greater home value) relative to the portfolio size heightens the likelihood of sustaining a positive portfolio balance. As a result, these strategies were shown to be more attractive in low-interest-rate environments. Evensky and company conclude that a standby line of credit deserves a role in mainstream retirement-income planning for four reasons:

1. It reduces the need to maintain a larger cash buffer;

2. It provides flexibility to hold on to investments during bear markets;

3. It allows flexibility to use home equity as a source of spending; and

4. It improves portfolio survivorship rates without an adverse impact on remaining legacy wealth.

In December 2013, the same authors returned with a second study on using a standby line of credit for retirement-income planning. This time, they shifted the focus to how much the sustainable withdrawal rate could be increased with a line of credit while maintaining a 90 percent success rate over a thirty-year retirement. They confirm that the standby line of credit helps sustain higher withdrawal rates when retirement starts in a low-interest-rate environment and/or the home is worth more than the investment portfolio.

Consistent with other withdrawal-rate research using lower capital-market expectations than the historical averages, they calculate that the sustainable spending rate without a reverse mortgage is 3.25 percent. With a reverse mortgage, the withdrawal rate can reach 6.5 percent. This highest number happens when the home value matches the portfolio size and interest rates are low at the start of retirement. They note that these higher withdrawal rates are on par with those obtained through dynamic spending strategies that can involve substantial spending reductions over time, but that the HECM strategy can sustain the higher spending rate without such reductions.

◉ Bringing the Reverse-Mortgage Tenure-Payment Option to the Forefront

December 2013 was a busy month for research articles on reverse mortgages in the *Journal of Financial Planning*. The other contribution published that month was Gerald Wagner's "The 6.0 Percent Rule." Based on the title alone, it would seem to provide only a further confirmation for the previous research that strategic use of a line of credit can enhance sustainability for higher spending rates.

However, this article provides an important further detail to the research to earn its place in the apex of this first generation of research from 2012 to 2013. Wagner contributes the idea that when there is an upward-sloping yield curve for interest rates (interest rates for long-term bonds are higher than for short-term bonds, which is the normal situation), setting up term or tenure payments with a reverse mortgage is even more effective than drawing down a line of credit in other ways. The tenure and term payments are based on a higher assumed interest rate with the ten-year LIBOR swap rate (plus the same lender's margin and mortgage-insurance premium as with line-of-credit growth), while the line of credit will grow at a rate based on the lower one-month LIBOR swap rate as the variable component. As long as short-term interest rates do not rise rapidly, tenure and term payments can be larger than a sustainable distribution level from the line of credit.

Term and tenure payments provide a different view of the line of credit. They provide fixed, ongoing payments for as long as the borrower remains in the home and eligible, or until the term finishes. A long life could lead to one being able to withdraw more than the principal limit, especially for tenure payments, as they continue even after the line of credit is exhausted. Term payments are calculated to avoid exhausting the line of credit, but an unexpected increase in interest rates could potentially cause the loan balance to exceed the principal limit. When this happens, full payments are guaranteed as well, for the length of the term and as long as the borrower remains in the home. My reverse-mortgage calculator allows users to determine the value of term and tenure payments from a reverse mortgage in addition to seeing the value of the line of credit that could be created.

◉ Putting It All Together

In April 2016, I published an article in the *Journal of Financial Planning* that outlined my own efforts to replicate these past research findings and to more deeply compare the different options for supporting retirement spending with a HECM. I've updated that research here to maintain the same assumptions used throughout the book. And for this second edition, I've updated the simulations based on the revised HECM rules in effect since October 2017. The starting point includes a ten-year LIBOR swap rate of 2.25 percent and a one-month LIBOR rate of 1.25 percent. Assuming a 2.25 percent lender's margin rate, this leads to an expected rate of 4.5 percent, which translates into a principal limit factor of 43.9 percent for a sixty-two-year-old borrower.

In the case study I developed, I also assumed a home value of $500,000 with no remaining mortgage. The example is based on the assumption that full up-front costs are paid without any credits. At loan origination, the initial mortgage-insurance premium to open the line of credit is 2 percent of the home value, or $10,000. I assume an origination cost of $6,000 and other closing costs of $2,500, for a combined total up-front cost of $18,500 when the loan is initiated. These are the full retail costs, but, again, shopping around may uncover opportunities for reduced origination fees and credits for some of the other cost components.

Except for the strategy in which the line of credit is drawn down first before spending from the investment portfolio, I assume that this initial cost is withdrawn from the portfolio rather than added to the loan balance.

The initial effective rate for principal limit growth adds the 1.25 percent one-month LIBOR rate to the 2.25 percent margin and the 0.5 percent ongoing mortgage-insurance premium, which is 4.0 percent initially. This variable rate will subsequently fluctuate based on simulated short-term interest rates, using my standard approach for developing Monte Carlo simulations that allows interest rates to gradually fluctuate toward their historical numbers, on average, over time.

The retiree in my study also holds $1 million in a tax-deferred investment portfolio. To provide a basic understanding about the impact of taxes, I applied a marginal tax rate of 25 percent to any portfolio distributions (distributions from the HECM reverse mortgage do not require any tax payments). The withdrawal rate reflects post-tax, inflation-adjusted spending goals as a percentage of the initial portfolio balance. For instance, a 4 percent withdrawal rate represents $40,000 of spending from the $1 million portfolio. The spending amount subsequently grows with the simulated inflation rate. If this distribution is taken from the portfolio, the withdrawal in real terms is $40,000 / (1 - 0.25) = $53,333 to cover taxes as well. If taken from the HECM alone, only $40,000 is needed.

Within each simulation, home prices and the HECM principal limit grow randomly in response to changing short-term interest rates. In each simulation, spending is sourced from the appropriate asset based on the rules for that strategy. When a strategy calls for spending from a depleted asset (the financial portfolio or HECM), the other asset is used instead when still available. Once both assets are depleted, shortfalls below the spending goal are tabulated in order to provide a negative legacy-wealth value. This is the real value of the spending shortfall without applying any investment returns or discount rates. Again, doing this is important to reflect the magnitude of potential failure with a strategy. I think it also provides a better basis for comparison.

I must admit that with the past research I described, I find it confusing to compare legacy values across different strategies, because they generally have retirees spending different amounts, and comparing results requires keeping track of both changes in spending and changes in legacy. I think that the results I describe now are internally consistent and more straightforward to compare, as they are all expressed for the same spending amounts, and the inclusion of a negative legacy provides a way to incorporate shortfalls relative to a spending goal.

Legacy wealth is calculated as the remaining portfolio balance plus any remaining home equity at the end of retirement. Remaining home equity is calculated as 95 percent of the home's appraised value at the end of retirement, less any balance due on the reverse-mortgage loan. Because of the nonrecourse features of the HECM program, remaining home equity cannot be negative, even if the loan balance exceeds the home's value.

Here are six retirement-spending strategies that use the investment portfolio and home equity in different ways:

1. *Home equity as last resort.* This strategy represents the conventional wisdom regarding home equity. It is the only home-equity strategy that delays opening a line of credit with a reverse mortgage. The investment portfolio is spent first. If and when the portfolio is depleted, a line of credit is opened with the reverse mortgage, and spending needs are then met with the line of credit until it is fully used. The PLF is calculated using the current PLF table for the updated age and simulated interest-rate value at the future date, assuming the same 2.25 percent lender's margin rate.

2. *Use home equity first.* This strategy opens the line of credit at the beginning of retirement, and retirement spending is covered from the line of credit first until it is fully used. This allows more time for the investment portfolio to grow before being used for withdrawals after the line of credit depletes.

3. *Sacks and Sacks coordination strategy.* This strategy opens the line of credit at the start of retirement and withdraws from it, when available, following any years in which the investment portfolio experienced a negative market return. No efforts are made to repay the loan balance until the full loan becomes due.

4. *Texas Tech coordination strategy.* This strategy is modified from the original strategy described by the Texas Tech University research

team (Evensky, Pfeiffer, and Salter) to remove the cash-reserve bucket. It performs a capital-needs analysis for the remaining portfolio wealth required to sustain the spending strategy over a forty-one-year time horizon. Spending is taken from the line of credit when possible—whenever the remaining portfolio balance is less than 80 percent of the required amount on the wealth glide path Otherwise, spending is taken from the investment portfolio. Whenever investment wealth rises above 80 percent of the glide-path value, any balance on the reverse mortgage is repaid as much as possible without letting wealth fall below the 80 percent threshold, in order to keep a lower loan balance over time and provide more growth potential for the line of credit, which was opened upon retirement.

5. *Use home equity last.* This strategy differs from the "home equity as last resort" strategy only in that the line of credit is opened at the start of retirement. It is otherwise not used and left to grow until the investment portfolio depletes.

6. *Use tenure payment.* This strategy uses the tenure-payment option on the full value of the available principal limit. With an initial home value of $500,000, an expected rate of 4.5 percent, and an age sixty-two start, annual tenure payments from the line of credit are $12,816. This amount does not adjust for inflation. The remainder of spending needs are covered by the investment portfolio for as long as financial assets remain.

Results are presented for each strategy, assuming an asset allocation of 50 percent stocks and 50 percent bonds. Results are displayed for years in retirement, allowing the retirement duration to be interpreted either as the date of death or the date the borrower leaves the home and must repay the reverse-mortgage loan balance.

To understand the implications of different strategies, Exhibit 6.1 shows the probability that the expenditure objectives for a 4 percent post-tax initial spending rate can continue to be met as retirement progresses. With a 25 percent marginal tax rate, this would imply a gross withdrawal rate of 5.33 percent in the first year of retirement if distributions are taken solely from the investment portfolio.

Exhibit 6.1

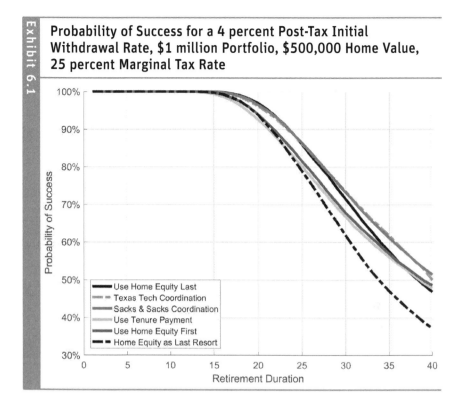

Probability of Success for a 4 percent Post-Tax Initial Withdrawal Rate, $1 million Portfolio, $500,000 Home Value, 25 percent Marginal Tax Rate

The six strategies are all comparable, because they all allow home equity to be used to meet spending goals alongside the investment portfolio. What differs among the strategies is the sequence for when to spend from the portfolio and when to spend from home equity.

The strategy supporting the lowest success rates for longer retirements is the conventional wisdom of using home equity as a last resort and initiating the reverse mortgage only after portfolio depletion has taken place. This confirms the original finding from the 2012 research article by Sacks and Sacks that launched this area of inquiry; the last-resort option is the worst way to coordinate the portfolio with a reverse mortgage for meeting retirement spending goals. It only benefits in terms of avoiding the need to pay up-front costs to set up the reverse mortgage for scenarios in which the investment portfolio performs well enough that home equity is not needed to meet spending goals.

The other five strategies generally support greater success by helping to ensure that spending can continue even when the portfolio does not perform well enough to support this alone. In the first edition, the "use home equity last" strategy for this comparison provided the highest increase in success rates. As a reminder, this is different from "home equity as a last resort," because this version of "use home equity last" opens the reverse mortgage at the start of retirement so that the line of credit can grow until it is first needed upon portfolio depletion. Otherwise, the two strategies are the same in that the reverse mortgage is used only after the portfolio depletes.

But now that principal limit growth has been slowed under the new rules, the benefits of the "use home equity last" strategy are weaker than before. The two coordinated strategies now support higher success rates than using home equity last. Their ability to provide ongoing support to mitigate sequence risk at inopportune times helps to offset the additional benefit from letting the line of credit grow for as long as possible before use. Meanwhile, the benefits from the other strategies (tenure payments, use home equity first) fall somewhere in between the two coordinated strategies and the home equity as last resort option.

It is also important to consider the combined legacy value of assets when using a reverse mortgage. Legacy value is defined as any remaining portfolio assets plus any remaining home equity after the reverse-mortgage loan balance has been repaid. If spendable assets are depleted (the portfolio and the entire line of credit) such that the full spending goal cannot be met, legacy values are counted as negative by summing the total spending shortfalls that would manifest either as reduced spending or as a need to rely on ones' heirs for additional support as a form of "reverse legacy." Once again, this addition of a negative legacy makes results more meaningful because it clarifies the magnitude to which a spending goal cannot be achieved. Legacy values are shown on an after-tax basis assuming that the same 25 percent marginal tax rate applies to portfolio assets, though the possibility of any tax deductions upon repaying the loan balance are not shown.

First, Exhibit 6.2 reveals that median legacy values when using different strategies remain close for much of the retirement period. The "home equity as a last resort" strategy provides a slight edge early on because the portfolio is not depleted until later, so this strategy simply saves on the up-front setup costs. However, later in retirement, a larger legacy

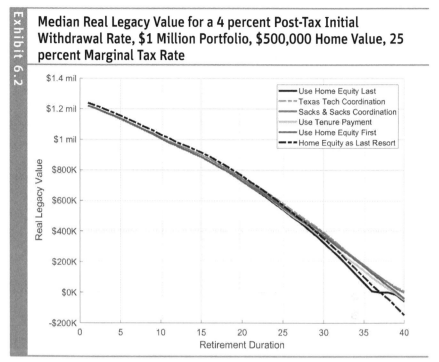

Exhibit 6.2

Median Real Legacy Value for a 4 percent Post-Tax Initial Withdrawal Rate, $1 Million Portfolio, $500,000 Home Value, 25 percent Marginal Tax Rate

Legend:
- Use Home Equity Last
- Texas Tech Coordination
- Sacks & Sacks Coordination
- Use Tenure Payment
- Use Home Equity First
- Home Equity as Last Resort

Y-axis: Real Legacy Value ($1.4 mil, $1.2 mil, $1 mil, $800K, $600K, $400K, $200K, $0K, -$200K)

X-axis: Retirement Duration (0, 5, 10, 15, 20, 25, 30, 35, 40)

is possible with other strategies. After forty years, the two coordinated strategies support the highest legacies, followed by using home equity first, the tenure-payment option, and using home equity last. Once portfolio depletion takes place, the last resort-option is not able to compete with the other strategies.

Next, Exhibit 6.3 shows the combined real legacy values at the ninetieth percentile of outcomes. These are cases when the investment portfolio performs extremely well throughout retirement. The exhibit demonstrates that if you can count on outsized investment returns, using the line of credit more quickly can be beneficial, as the portfolio grows more quickly than the loan balance.

Using home equity first, the tenure strategy, and the Sacks and Sacks coordination strategy all lean toward a quicker use of home equity than the other strategies, which support higher combined legacy values.

Next is the last-resort option, which is located where it is because of its ability to save on ever having to pay the up-front costs for a reverse mortgage line of credit that will not otherwise ever be used, because markets performed so well. The final two strategies open the line of credit

Exhibit 6.3

90th Percentile Real Legacy Value for a 4 percent Post-Tax Initial Withdrawal Rate, $1 Million Portfolio, $500,000 Home Value, 25 percent Marginal Tax Rate

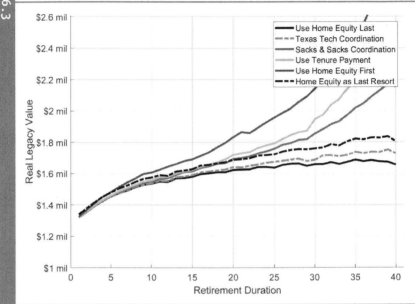

Exhibit 6.4

10th Percentile Real Legacy Value for a 4 percent Post-Tax Initial Withdrawal Rate, $1 Million Portfolio, $500,000 Home Value, 25 percent Marginal Tax Rate

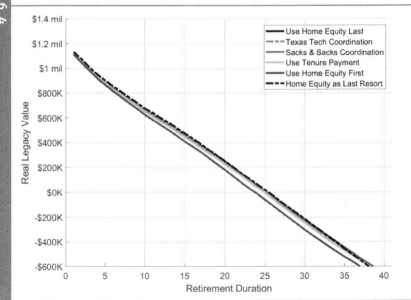

initially but end up using it very rarely, if at all, and so these provide the smallest relative advantages for legacy value.

Finally, while Exhibit 6.3 shows what happens when markets perform extremely well, Exhibit 6.4 shows results for the tenth percentile of outcomes—when market performance is poor. These are the bad-luck cases for market returns and sequence risk, in which planning generally focuses on providing a workable solution. In such cases, legacy values reach $0 by about twenty-five years into retirement. Spending down home equity first becomes the riskiest strategy, as the delay in taking distributions from the portfolio has not sufficiently helped if the portfolio has not grown adequately in the meantime. In the first edition, strategies that delayed the use of home equity allowed for greater opportunities to benefit from the nonrecourse aspects of the loans by preventing negative legacies for longer. Those simulations are still relevant for applications made before October 2, 2017. But the new rules that slow principal limit growth have removed these opportunities for new borrowers. These strategies now all transition smoothly into providing negative legacies after about twenty-five years.

◎ Summary

Strategies that spend the home equity more quickly increase the overall risk for the retirement plan. More upside potential is generated by delaying the need to take distributions from investments, but more downside risk is created because the home equity is used quickly without necessarily being compensated for by sufficiently high market returns.

For other strategies that tend to delay home-equity use, there are two potential mechanisms by which the HECM can provide benefits. First, strategic spending from the reverse mortgage throughout retirement can help to manage sequence-of-returns risk by reducing the need for portfolio distributions at inopportune times. The Sacks and Sacks and the Texas Tech coordination strategies best represent this benefit.

Second, the growing line of credit with the HECM can allow for greater future spending that even provides a potential to benefit from the nonrecourse aspects of the loan when the line of credit is still available and the loan balance has exceeded the home value. Using home equity last best reflects this benefit.

In the first edition, the benefits of the growing line of credit were stronger than the synergistic benefits of managing sequence risk with a coordinated strategy. However, with the presentation in this new edition, the coordinated strategies now have an edge in providing better overall performance because the principal limit generally starts from a lower level and grows more slowly than before. This weakens the benefits of just letting the line of credit grow and not drawing from it strategically throughout retirement.

For readers not wishing to manage the complexities of using one of the coordinated strategies, the simple tenure-payment option can also serve retirees well. It provides an ongoing monthly payment that helps to reduce portfolio distributions, which is another way to help mitigate sequence risk. These monthly payments continue for as long as the borrower remains eligible for the loan, even in the rare event that tenure payments have fully depleted the line of credit.

Further Reading

Pfau, Wade D. 2016. "Incorporating Home Equity into a Retirement Income Strategy." *Journal of Financial Planning* 29 (4): 41–49.

Pfeiffer, Shaun, C. Angus Schaal, and John Salter. 2014. "HECM Reverse Mortgages: Now or Last Resort?" *Journal of Financial Planning* 27 (5): 44–51.

Pfeiffer, Shaun, John R. Salter, and Harold R. Evensky. 2013. "Increasing the Sustainable Withdrawal Rate Using the Standby Reverse Mortgage." *Journal of Financial Planning* 26 (12): 55–62.

Sacks, Barry H., and Stephen R. Sacks. 2012. "Reversing the Conventional Wisdom: Using Home Equity to Supplement Retirement Income." *Journal of Financial Planning* 25 (2): 43–52.

Salter, John R., Shaun A. Pfeiffer, and Harold R. Evensky. 2012. "Standby Reverse Mortgages: A Risk Management Tool for Retirement Distributions." *Journal of Financial Planning* 25 (8): 40–48.

Wagner, Gerald C. 2013. "The 6.0 Percent Rule." *Journal of Financial Planning* 26 (12): 46–59.

CHAPTER 7

Funding Source for Retirement Efficiency Improvements

A reverse mortgage may be a helpful resource to support certain long-term strategies that require paying short-term costs to obtain long-term gains, such as:

- to create a Social Security delay bridge;
- to use the tenure-payment option as an alternative to purchasing an income annuity;
- to use the reverse mortgage as an alternative source of longevity insurance;
- to pay for the taxes to enable Roth conversions in the years prior to required minimum distributions;
- to otherwise help manage falling into a higher-than- necessary tax bracket; or
- to maintain an existing long-term care insurance policy by paying insurance premiums from the line of credit.

For those with sufficient assets who could afford to fund these retirement efficiencies with their investment portfolios, the matter becomes determining the direction that can provide the most attractive distribution of overall outcomes for the retirement plan. Applying these sorts of strategies would become a subset of general uses for a HECM to support retirement spending in the most efficient manner.

This chapter provides a detailed focus on using a reverse mortgage to support Social Security delay or as a replacement for an income annuity.

◉ Building a Social Security Delay Bridge

In the first edition of this book, I did not go into elaborate detail about using a reverse mortgage to help support the short-term costs of delaying Social Security. This is what I wrote:

> [Funding a delay of Social Security through a reverse mortgage] may have the biggest impact for typical Americans approaching age sixty-two with few financial assets and most of their net worth tied up in their home. For example, those with a small enough investment portfolio and who cannot work past sixty-two may not otherwise be able to afford to delay Social Security. Home equity could provide a way to build that bridge to Social Security delay. For some individuals, though, the available principal limit from the reverse mortgage may be insufficient to support eight years of age seventy benefits, or even age sixty-two benefits. There would be also be an important trade-off to consider, as the housing asset on the balance sheet would be diminished to fund Social Security delay, which leaves fewer contingency assets available to the household. The guaranteed lifetime income stream supported through Social Security would be dramatically enhanced though. It would be important to explore these possibilities and trade-offs on a case-by-case basis to determine the best course of action.

More elaborate detail on this matter is now needed on account of a poorly prepared report issued by the Consumer Financial Protection Bureau (CFPB) in August 2017 that makes it seem like using a reverse mortgage to delay Social Security is a bad idea across the board. This report gained a lot of press coverage and is likely serving as the primary resource for people seeking to learn more about the matter.

To begin, I am not philosophically opposed to the CFPB. I have served as an intern at the Social Security Administration, and my original career goal, before finding my place in academics, was to become a US government economist. So, I am more disappointed than anything else that this report was issued and heralded with a press release and other promotion by the CFPB.

However, there is a line in the conclusion of the report that makes sense: "For consumers who have the option, working past age sixty-two is usually a less costly way to increase their monthly Social Security benefit than borrowing from a reverse mortgage." This is true. Delaying retirement is probably the best possible way to build stronger finances for retirement. But for those who have retired at sixty-two, what is the best way to coordinate Social Security claims, home equity, and the investment portfolio to build an efficient overall retirement-income plan? The report fails to answer this adequately; its efforts to say that a reverse mortgage is too costly is incomplete.

What the report does is to estimate the increase in total Social Security benefits (ignoring cost-of-living adjustments) obtained through a life expectancy of eighty-five by waiting until age sixty-seven to claim Social Security benefits. Technically, this is not a delay of Social Security; it is just claiming at the article's assumed full retirement age rather than early. The additional benefits are compared to the costs of replacing those five years of "missing" benefits by taking distributions from a HECM line of credit. Reverse-mortgage costs consist of the up-front fees, insurance premiums, servicing costs, and interest accumulated at the age-eighty-five life expectancy, which the article shows are substantially higher than the net gain in Social Security benefits, leading the authors to conclude:

> We find that borrowing a reverse mortgage loan to get an increased Social Security benefit carries significant costs that generally exceed the additional lifetime amount gained from delaying Social Security. In addition, the amount that a consumer will need to borrow from a reverse mortgage loan to delay claiming Social Security benefits could negatively affect the consumer's ability to move or use their home equity to meet a large expense later in life.

These conclusions violate two of the tenets of my Retirement Researcher Manifesto outlined in chapter 1. First, tenet (1) is to play the long game. We should not base our decisions about what happens at life expectancy but rather what happens if we live well beyond it. Delaying Social Security is a form of insurance that helps to support the increasing costs associated with living a long life. It provides inflation-adjusted lifetime benefits for a retiree and a surviving spouse, and these lifetime benefits will be 76 percent larger in inflation-adjusted terms for those who claim at seventy instead of at sixty-two. The value of this insurance is missed when analysis only considers the impacts through life expectancy.

Second, and more important, the CFPB report authors have violated tenet (7), which involves working with the entire retirement balance sheet and matching assets to liabilities. We do not know the liabilities to be funded in the CFPB report; there is no given spending goal to be achieved. The report also completely ignores the possible existence of an investment portfolio to help fund retirement. If retirees have expenses to meet, they must draw from their assets. For someone retired at sixty-two, how will expenses be met? Should retirees claim Social Security early? Or build a bridge to delay Social Security using a reverse mortgage? Or delay Social Security but fund the delay instead through distributions from an investment portfolio?

The CFPB report does not address this issue at all. All the report really seems to say is that it is better to work longer and to not retire at sixty-two. This allows expenses to be covered by labor income. Fair enough; this is the best decision to bolster finances. But it simply does not address what people should do when they stop working before seventy. The CFPB's notion that the costs of a reverse mortgage exceed the benefits of Social Security delay is incomplete because it does not address how to fund the spending need other than to assume that a person is still working. If retired, distributions from an investment portfolio also have a cost in terms of the lost compounding growth potential for those funds if they are spent instead of remaining in the portfolio.

Saying that using a reverse mortgage is too costly because it could hurt the ability to move or to use home equity for another expense ignores asset-liability matching for the retirement-spending goal. Meeting spending needs from the investment portfolio instead could potentially drain net worth faster than meeting spending needs from the reverse mortgage. We have to test this to see which strategy can best preserve net worth after retirement expenses are met, so that more liquidity is available later in retirement to fund a move or other expensive shock. Again, the CFPB report ignores both the spending goal and the investment portfolio, so it does not provide any meaningful conclusions about what a retiree at sixty-two should do.

Properly addressing this requires a more complete analysis than the CFPB report provides. We can analyze these complexities with regard to long-term impacts and asset-liability matching by using my standard approach for developing Monte Carlo simulations that allows interest rates to start at their lower current levels and gradually fluctuate toward their historical averages over time. When it comes to the Social Security claim decision, we consider four options for those entering retirement at age sixty-two and no longer working:

1. Delay claiming Social Security benefits until age seventy; open a HECM at age sixty-two and draw the equivalent amount of the age sixty-two Social Security benefit (without cost-of-living adjustments) from the line of credit to replace these missing benefits. Once Social Security begins at age seventy, stop distributions from the HECM. To reduce the loan balance and transfer more of the principal limit back to the line of credit for use if the investment portfolio later depletes, make a voluntary repayment to reduce the loan balance by the amount of the original age sixty-two benefit without cost-of-living adjustments in years after positive market returns and when at least two years of the retirement-spending goal remains in the investment portfolio. Use any remaining line of credit as a spending source if the investment portfolio depletes later in retirement.

2. Delay claiming Social Security benefits until age seventy; open a HECM at age sixty-two and draw the equivalent amount of the age sixty-two Social Security benefit (without cost-of-living adjustments) from the line of credit to replace these missing benefits. Once Social Security begins at age seventy, stop distributions from the HECM. Do not voluntarily pay down the HECM loan balance. Use any remaining line of credit as a spending source if the investment portfolio depletes later in retirement.

3. Delay claiming Social Security benefits until age seventy. Draw the full amount of the retirement-spending goal from the investment portfolio. This requires larger distributions for the first eight years of retirement, but distributions reduce by the amount of the Social Security benefit once it begins at age seventy. Open a HECM only as a last-resort option to meet the spending goal if the investment portfolio depletes later in retirement.

4. Begin Social Security benefits at age sixty-two. Draw the remaining amount needed to meet the overall retirement-spending goal from the investment portfolio. Open a HECM only as a last-resort option to meet the spending goal if the investment portfolio depletes later in retirement.

Let's do a case study with a sixty-two-year-old single individual entering retirement. She owns a home appraised at $400,000 as well as a tax-deferred retirement account with $1 million of assets. The investment portfolio uses a fifty-fifty asset allocation for stocks and bonds.

Her full retirement age for Social Security is sixty-six, and at that age she is eligible for a benefit equal to $2,000 per month, or $24,000 per year. If she claims early at sixty-two, her lifetime benefit is reduced to $18,000 per year, and if she delays Social Security to seventy, her yearly benefit increases to $31,880 in inflation-adjusted terms. Without including inflation adjustments, eight years of her age sixty-two Social Security benefits sum to $144,000.

Her spending goal to be covered by her investment portfolio, home equity, and Social Security is $50,000 per year before taxes, and this grows with inflation. She has other pension income such that we assume for this portion of assets, she is in the 25 percent marginal tax bracket, and 85 percent of her Social Security benefits as well as any investment-portfolio distributions will count as taxable income. We do not consider required minimum distributions from the qualified plan, which may accelerate the need to pay taxes and force some of her assets into a taxable account in simulations where markets perform well.

At retirement, she considers a HECM with a lender's margin of 2.25 percent when the ten-year LIBOR swap rate is 2.25 percent. For a sixty-two-year-old, this translates into an initial PLF of 43.9 percent, with the expected rate of 4.5 percent. Up-front costs include a $6,000 origination fee, an initial mortgage-insurance premium of 2 percent of the home value, plus another $2,500 for other closing costs. These costs total $16,500. (Again, it should be clear that this represents the full retail price to avoid biasing the results in favor of the reverse mortgage; I've noted that borrowers can shop around for waivers and credits of such fees and costs.)

In this case study, the up-front costs are financed within the loan. This leaves a net initial principal limit of $159,100 (400,000 x 0.439 – 16,500). In cases where the reverse mortgage is opened later, I assume that the maximum eligible home value (currently $679,650) and the closing costs rise with inflation.

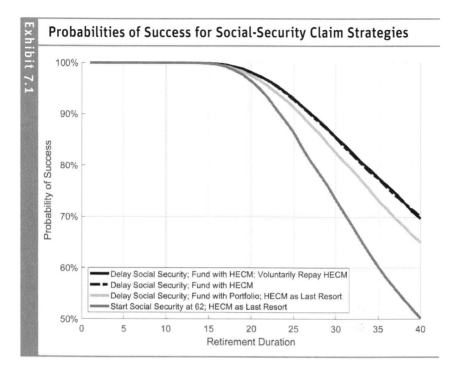

Probabilities of Success for Social-Security Claim Strategies

Exhibit 7.1

Probability of Success

Retirement Duration

Legend:
- Delay Social Security; Fund with HECM; Voluntarily Repay HECM
- Delay Social Security; Fund with HECM
- Delay Social Security; Fund with Portfolio; HECM as Last Resort
- Start Social Security at 62; HECM as Last Resort

Exhibit 7.1 provides the results for this case study in terms of the ongoing probability of success in meeting the spending goal throughout retirement. Claiming Social Security at sixty-two and opening the HECM only as a last-resort option if the portfolio depletes results in the lowest probabilities of success. There is value in spending down other resources (either investments or home equity) during the first eight years of retirement in order to enjoy a permanently higher Social Security benefit after that point.

Moving toward better outcomes, the next strategy is to delay Social Security to seventy and spend from the investment portfolio in the meantime, and then open a HECM only as a last-resort option if the investment portfolio depletes. Thirty years into retirement, this method has raised the probability of success from 72 percent to 82 percent. Higher distributions needed in the first eight years of retirement are more than offset by the larger benefits subsequently available at age seventy, such that the overall probability of success increases.

Next, the two strategies supporting the highest success rates both involve delaying Social Security and funding the delay through distributions from a HECM rather than distributions from the investment portfolio. This affirms that even after accounting for the full retail costs of setting up a reverse mortgage, this method's ability to help reduce sequence risk for the portfolio provides greater net advantages. It is interesting, however, that voluntarily paying down reverse-mortgage debt after age seventy to transfer a portion of the growing principal limit from loan balance to line of credit does not have a noticeable impact on success rates. After thirty years, both strategies have raised the success rate for this spending goal to about 85 percent.

We can also consider legacy wealth. This is the value of legacy assets available to heirs. It is defined as any remaining portfolio assets after taxes plus any remaining home equity after the reverse mortgage loan balance has been repaid. Exhibit 7.2 shows the legacy value of assets at the median outcome (which, we've noted, means that half of the values will be less than shown and half will be greater). The median reflects an average or typical outcome. Claiming at age sixty-two supports more legacy until about twenty to twenty-five years into retirement (ages eighty-two to eighty-seven). After that time, delay strategies all help to support greater legacy because the higher Social Security benefits help to dramatically reduce remaining distribution needs. Using the portfolio to delay does come out slightly ahead, but the reverse-mortgage strategies remain competitive. The possibility for lower up-front costs on the reverse mortgage may close much of this gap. Compared to claiming at sixty-two, which the CFPB report seemingly endorses in the absence of continued work, Social Security delay strategies help dramatically to provide legacy for longer and costlier retirements when dollars of legacy will have a bigger impact for heirs.

An unlucky outcome is represented by the tenth percentile for legacy wealth. Portfolio returns are poor, and the financial portfolio is quickly depleted. I have not included an exhibit to show this case, because it looks similar to the median case except that wealth depletion happens sooner. Claiming at sixty-two depletes available assets by age eighty-eight, and then it leaves a smaller Social Security benefit after that point as a remaining source for retirement income.

Using a reverse mortgage to fund Social Security delay can help support the full spending goal for another year, and funding the delay by spending from the investment portfolio helps support the full spending goal until age ninety-one. With these delay strategies, the Social Security benefit

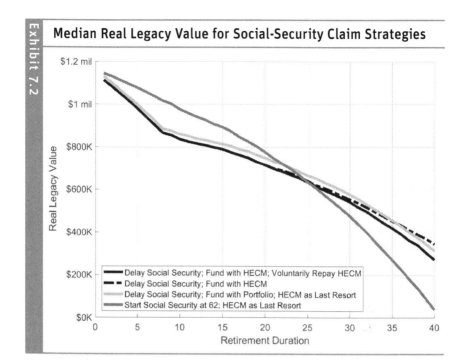

Exhibit 7.2

Median Real Legacy Value for Social-Security Claim Strategies

Real Legacy Value

$1.2 mil
$1 mil
$800K
$600K
$400K
$200K
$0K

Delay Social Security; Fund with HECM; Voluntarily Repay HECM
Delay Social Security; Fund with HECM
Delay Social Security; Fund with Portfolio; HECM as Last Resort
Start Social Security at 62; HECM as Last Resort

0   5   10   15   20   25   30   35   40
Retirement Duration

provides 76 percent more spending power after the investment portfolio and home equity are no longer able to contribute to retirement spending.

The ninetieth percentile for legacy values is shown in Exhibit 7.3, where the investment portfolio performs well, and distributions can continue indefinitely without depleting the portfolio. The portfolio is able to grow at a faster rate than the principal limit, and so, retirees benefit over the long term and keep more assets in their investment portfolio by spending from the HECM more quickly. The higher subsequent portfolio value more than offsets the growing loan balance for the HECM. Claiming at age sixty-two supports more legacy for about twenty-five years. Over the long term, funding Social Security delay with the HECM supports greater legacy, followed by funding delay through the investment portfolio.

Contrary to conclusions made in the CFPB report, there is value in supporting Social Security delay by spending down other resources in the interim. Spending from the HECM or an investment portfolio are both viable options to support a higher probability of success and a greater legacy value for assets over the long term. It is not the case that using a HECM to fund Social Security delay creates greater risk for retirees

Exhibit 7.3

90th Percentile Legacy Value for Social-Security Claim Strategies

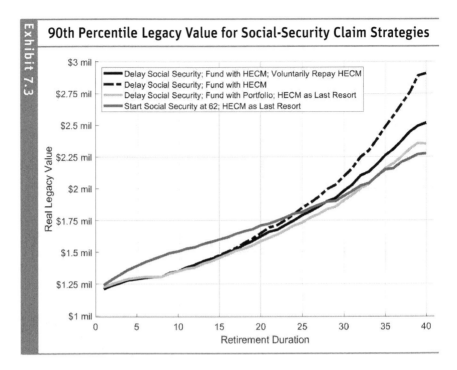

experiencing spending shocks or needing to move later in retirement, because reduced distribution needs from the investment portfolio and the aid this provides for reducing sequence risk help offset reverse-mortgage costs and preserve overall net worth.

⊙ The Tenure Option as an Annuity Alternative

When comparing different strategies for coordinating home equity with portfolio distributions to generate retirement income, the tenure option fares well. As a way to fund retirement efficiency improvements, using the tenure-payment option from the line of credit as an alternative to purchasing an income annuity is worth exploring further. The tenure option "annuitizes" home equity as an alternative to annuitizing financial assets. If you are considering income annuities as you approach retirement, what could be a more effective way to build an income stream: purchasing an income annuity, or using a tenure-payment option on a reverse mortgage? The tenure option behaves similarly to an income annuity, though they are not the same.

First, to be clear, a tenure payment does not necessarily provide a guaranteed monthly cash flow for life as an income annuity would.

Guaranteed cash flow continues only as long as the borrower remains eligible for the loan by staying in the home and meeting homeowner obligations. Moving away from the home for more than a year would end the payments. While an eligible nonborrowing spouse may remain in the home if the borrower is no longer eligible, tenure payments stop once the borrower has become ineligible. Only when both spouses are eligible borrowers would the tenure payment behave like a joint-life annuity.

Another important difference is that no lump-sum payment (other than the up-front reverse-mortgage costs) must be given up from the investment portfolio to initiate the tenure payments. Each tenure payment is taken from the line of credit and moved to the loan balance as it is received. In the event that the retiree dies early, the loan balance may be substantially less than an annuity premium would have been. Conceptually, the tenure payment behaves more closely to an income annuity with a cash-refund provision, in terms of whether any assets are available at the end of the contract period. Still, there is no up-front, lump-sum premium to initiate these payments with the tenure option. This is an important distinction that allows the tenure payment to further preserve investment assets.

The tenure payment also does not provide mortality credits in a conventional sense. Mortality credits are part of an income-annuity payment; they are the subsidies paid by the short-lived in the risk pool to the long-lived. Tenure-payment pricing is based on an assumption that the borrower or borrowers live to age one hundred. Despite the lack of traditional mortality credits, tenure payments provide a degree of longevity protection, assuming the borrower remains eligible. Cash flow received from the line of credit through the tenure payment can exceed the value of the principal limit and can even exceed the value of the home. As I've noted, once this happens, the nonrecourse aspects of the loan provide spending power without a trade-off to legacy in a way philosophically similar to how an income annuity can continue to provide payments to the long-lived that well exceed the premium amount and interest. That nonrecourse aspect could be interpreted as a type of "mortality credit."

A final difference is between the formulas that calculate tenure payments and income-annuity payments. As discussed before, the tenure payout rate depends on the ten-year LIBOR swap rate plus a lender's margin and a mortgage-insurance premium rate of 0.5 percent. It also depends on an assumed time horizon or "life expectancy" of age one hundred. It does not vary by gender or whether payments are for one or two eligible borrowers.

Meanwhile, an income annuity depends on actual mortality data for the age and gender of the individual or couple, as well as on a lower interest rate that may be a bit higher than a ten-year LIBOR swap rate because of its link to corporate bond yields, but it doesn't include a lender's margin or mortgage-insurance premium in its calculation.

For the tenure payment, the higher interest rate helps support higher payments than those from an income annuity. But the assumption that "life expectancy" is age one hundred supports lower payments relative to the income annuity. It is not clear in advance whether the higher-interest-rate assumption will counterbalance the age one hundred assumption, such that the implied payout rate from the tenure payment is more or less than that of the income annuity.

For example, as I write, the ten-year LIBOR swap rate is about 2.25 percent. For a tenure payment to a sixty-five-year-old with a lender's margin of 2.25 percent, the payout rate for the tenure payment option is 5.44 percent. This is calculated as a monthly tenure payment of $624 on a $300,000 house for a sixty-five year-old financing the full up-front costs of $13,500. The payout rate is the $7,491 of annual income from the tenure payment as a percentage of the $137,700 initial principal limit (45.9 percent of $300,000). We can compare this rate to annuity quotes with cash refunds offered through ImmediateAnnuities.com for sixty-five-year-olds. The payout is 6.59 percent for a single male, 5.82 percent for a female, and 5.39 percent for couples. The tenure payment offers a lower payout rate except for the case of a couple purchasing a joint-income annuity. Women and couples benefit from the tenure payment on a relative basis, as it does not penalize them for their longer relative life expectancies.

Another interesting aspect to consider for tenure payments is that, surprisingly, the monthly tenure payment amount for a given home value decreases as interest rates rise, at least for expected rates in excess of 3.5 percent. Higher interest rates allow for a higher payout rate from the principal limit amount as just discussed. This is documented at the top of Exhibit 7.4 for expected rates between 3 percent and 10 percent, in the case of a sixty-five-year-old borrower with a $300,000 home. The

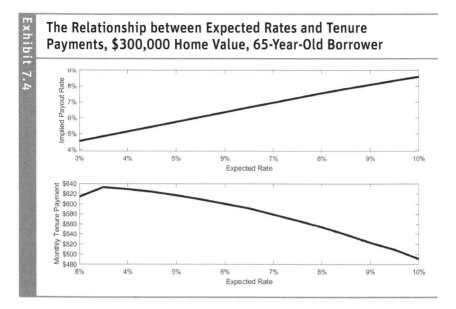

Exhibit 7.4

The Relationship between Expected Rates and Tenure Payments, $300,000 Home Value, 65-Year-Old Borrower

payout rate from the principal limit increases from 4.53 percent when the expected rate is 3 percent, to 8.58 percent when the expected rate is 10 percent. However, the initial principal limit that the payout rate is applied to decreases as rates rise, creating a stronger counter-effect. For a sixty-five-year-old borrower, an expected rate of 3 percent supports a principal limit factor of 54.2 percent. The principal limit factor falls to 22.9 percent when the expected rate is 10 percent. Overall monthly tenure payments fall from $614 to $491 with this rate increase. The surprising implication is that tenure payments will represent a higher percentage of the home's value when interest rates are low.

With income annuities, a given lump-sum premium would support a larger monthly payment when interest rates are higher. Of course, the principal limit rather than the home value would provide an equivalent amount to annuitize, but the interesting point is that low interest rates allow for more annuitized spending from home equity for a household with a given ratio of home value to portfolio size.

About whether to choose tenure payments or income annuities, Exhibit 7.5 describes circumstances that would favor one or the other. First, as noted, couples and single females would experience lower payout rates from income annuities, as their pricing considers their increased longevity relative to single males. Single males can receive the highest relative payout rates from income annuities and would have a stronger reason to consider them, relatively speaking. Second, tenure payments make more sense for those planning to remain in their homes, as they have more opportunity to spread out any up-front costs and potentially receive a windfall from the nonrecourse aspect of tenure payments. For those likely to move or who otherwise do not live in an eligible home, income annuities have an edge.

Next, for those with less risk aversion, tenure payments are worth considering as a way to obtain more guaranteed cash flows without having to take dollars out of the stock market. For income annuities, I suggest treating the annuitized assets as part of your bond holdings, but in practice this can be difficult, because the remaining investment portfolio becomes more stock-heavy and volatile. In practice, real-world considerations probably mean that partial annuitization will also reduce stock holdings for most retirees, but the full portfolio and original asset allocation can remain intact more easily with the tenure-payment option.

Next, as noted, in a low-interest-rate environment, a given home value can support a higher tenure payment than otherwise. This gives tenure payments an edge to provide more spending power for a given home value to financial portfolio ratio, relative to income annuities. Finally, the tenure payments are not added to adjustable gross income, whereas annuity income is subject to taxes when initiated from either tax-deferred or taxable resources.

Tenure payments have many favorable characteristics. A tenure payment allows for an annuitized spending stream generated by home equity, subject to the caveat that it may not last for life if the borrower moves

Exhibit 7.5	Circumstances Favoring Tenure Payments or Income Annuities	
	Tenure Payment	**Income Annuity**
	• Couples	• Single male
	• Plan to remain in eligible home	• Likely to move; live in ineligible home
	• Less risk averse	• More risk averse
	• Shorter life expectancy	• Longer life expectancy
	• Low-interest-rate environment	• High-interest-rate environment
	• Being subject to high tax rates	• Being subject to low tax rates

or cannot maintain the home. It does not require assets to be extracted as a large lump-sum annuity premium. For individuals uncomfortable with increasing their stock allocation for remaining assets after partial annuitization, the tenure payment option would allow more assets to remain in the stock market and focused on growth with a lower portfolio stock allocation.

Simulating Tenure and Income-Annuity Options

There has been research providing simulations to quantify these comparisons. Joe Tomlinson, a financial planner in Maine, initiated work on comparing reverse-mortgage options and income annuities with a column he wrote for *Advisor Perspectives* in April 2015. He followed that up with more detailed joint research with John Salter and Shaun Pfeiffer for an article published in the Spring 2016 issue of the *Journal of Personal Finance*. Two of the options compared are relevant for our discussion: initiating tenure payments with a reverse mortgage, and purchasing enough income annuity to obtain the same payments as the tenure option could provide while also opening a line of credit on the reverse mortgage and using it only if needed later in life.

Tomlinson, Salter, and Pfeiffer found that longevity-protected cash flows can enhance retirement spending, even compared to a strategy of opening a line of credit and delaying its use. The researchers further found evidence that using home equity can provide greater spending support than carving out a portion of assets to purchase an income annuity. They considered scenarios when interest rates remain low and when they rise shortly after retirement begins, after the reverse-mortgage and income-annuity decisions have already been made.

Compared to buying an income annuity and opening a line of credit, the tenure-payment option supports more spending on average as well as a larger average legacy. These outcomes also hold if interest rates subsequently rise, though the differences are smaller, as the line of credit can grow faster and support more spending later in the case that an income annuity is combined with opening a line of credit. The tenure-payment option allows more dollars to remain in the stock market, which helps, on average.

On the downside, the income-annuity strategy provided more income at the fifth percentile of the distribution, especially if interest rates rise in the future. This finding is contingent upon opening the line of credit at the start of retirement when also annuitizing, and then delaying the line-of-credit use until the portfolio is depleted.

The research approach used by Tomlinson's team differs a bit from my usual approach. They track the amount of spending that could be generated by different strategies, while I tend to focus on how well different strategies are able to meet a fixed spending objective and what sorts of shortfalls may arise in the effort to meet it. I have created an analysis along these lines and can confirm their general findings that the tenure option can provide a potentially attractive alternative to partial annuitization. After the October 2, 2017, rule change, tenure payments are no longer clearly superior to income annuities; both become competitive options.

Consider a scenario similar to the one we used to compare different portfolio-coordination strategies in chapter 6: a couple reaches age sixty-five with a $500,000 home and $1 million in tax-deferred retirement plans. In addition to income from Social Security and other sources, they would like to fund another $40,000 from their assets in inflation-adjusted and after-tax terms. They are in the 25 percent marginal tax bracket (this is the tax rate they pay on distributions from their investment assets). To meet their $40,000 spending objective, they need to withdraw enough to also cover taxes. They would need $53,333 from their retirement plan to have $40,000 left after taxes. But since reverse-mortgage distributions are not taxable income, a $40,000 distribution would cover their need.

I consider a HECM when the ten-year LIBOR swap rate is 2.25 percent and with a margin rate of 2.25 percent. This leads to a PLF of 45.9 percent and a principal limit of $229,500. With up-front costs totaling $18,500 paid from the loan balance, the available annual tenure payments for this HECM loan add to $12,726. For income annuities, the couple uses ImmediateAnnuities.com to find a joint-life annuity with fixed lifetime payments and a cash-refund provision that has a payout rate of 5.37 percent. A life-only version has a payout of 5.53 percent, but the cash-refund provision makes the income more comparable to how the legacy cost of tenure payments would be determined, with each tenure payment added to the loan balance as it is received. The couple is also comfortable with an asset allocation of 50 percent stocks and 50 percent bonds for their investment portfolio.

I consider four scenarios for using reverse mortgages and income annuities as part of the retirement-income plan:

1. *Investments only.* The couple does not purchase an income annuity and opens a reverse mortgage only as a last-resort option in the event that the investment portfolio is depleted.

2. *Tenure payment.* The couple uses the tenure payment for a HECM, which provides $12,726 annually without inflation adjustments. This represents 5.54 percent of the principal limit. Any remaining funds needed to meet spending objectives are taken as distributions from the investment portfolio.

3. *Income annuity purchased proportionately from investments.* The couple takes $229,500 (the equivalent initial principal limit amount) from the retirement account and purchases a joint-life income annuity with cash refund offering a payout rate of 5.37 percent. This supports $12,324 of annual income before taxes, or $9,243 after taxes are paid. For assets remaining in the investment portfolio, the couple maintains an allocation of 50 percent stocks and 50 percent bonds. A HECM line of credit is opened only as a last-resort option later in retirement if the portfolio is depleted.

4. *Income annuity purchased as bond alternative.* The couple takes $229,500 from the retirement account and purchases a joint-life income annuity. This is the same as the previous scenario except that this purchase is made with only bonds, so the stock allocation for the remaining investment portfolio increases because the amount of stocks remains as before. The new asset allocation for remaining investments is 65 percent stocks and 35 percent bonds. A HECM line of credit is opened only as a last-resort option later in retirement if the portfolio is depleted.

The next exhibits provide the results for these four strategies, beginning with the probability of success in Exhibit 7.6. Compared to the strategy that does not use an income annuity and only leaves a reverse mortgage as

Exhibit 7.6

Probability of Success for Tenure-Payment and Income-Annuity Strategies

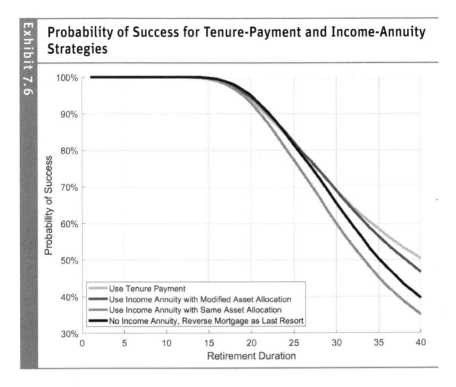

a last resort option, strategies using income annuities or tenure payments support higher probabilities of success. The two strategies competing to provide the best outcome are the use of a tenure payment as an alternative to the income annuity, or using an income annuity with the premium payment drawn from bonds (modified asset allocation).

Both of these strategies are competitive in supporting higher success rates, with a slight edge for the tenure-payment option with the longest retirements. Income annuities provide similar underlying investment returns as bonds, and after life expectancy, they provide a unique source of additional returns in the form of mortality credits. These mortality credits explain the improved performance when the amount of stocks held is allowed to remain the same at retirement. The tenure-payment option is also a winner among these choices. It consistently supports a higher probability of success by leaving more in the investment portfolio, by supporting spending without adding to adjusted gross income, and by reducing portfolio distributions and sequence-of-returns risk. A retiree may wish to consider either a tenure payment or an income annuity as ways to help improve success rates for a longer retirement compared to strategies that more fully rely on drawing from an investment portfolio throughout retirement.

In Exhibit 7.7, we track median inflation-adjusted legacy wealth over time. Here, legacy wealth consists of remaining investment assets, remaining home equity after loan repayment, and any cash refund on the income annuity in the event of an early death. The tenure-payment option is competitive in supporting the largest legacy value of assets at the median throughout the retirement horizon, though the income annuity drawn from bonds (modified asset allocation) and relying only on the investment portfolio both perform at a similar level. The worst outcome in this exhibit is the partial annuitization case when the amount of stocks held is reduced, because the asset allocation remains the same after partial annuitization. In the median outcome, holding less in stocks and missing the realized upside hurts legacy outcomes.

Finally, Exhibit 7.8 provides outcomes at the ninetieth percentile when markets perform exceptionally well. Again, the tenure-payment option consistently remains competitive, though legacy is frequently even larger

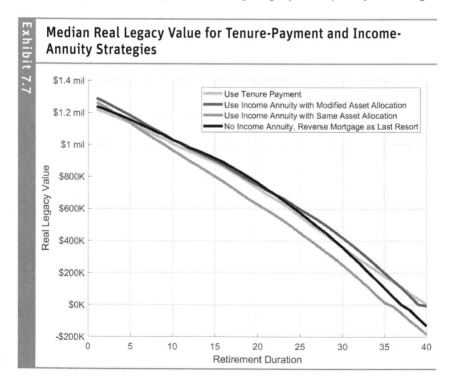

Exhibit 7.7

Median Real Legacy Value for Tenure-Payment and Income-Annuity Strategies

Use Tenure Payment
Use Income Annuity with Modified Asset Allocation
Use Income Annuity with Same Asset Allocation
No Income Annuity, Reverse Mortgage as Last Resort

Real Legacy Value

Retirement Duration

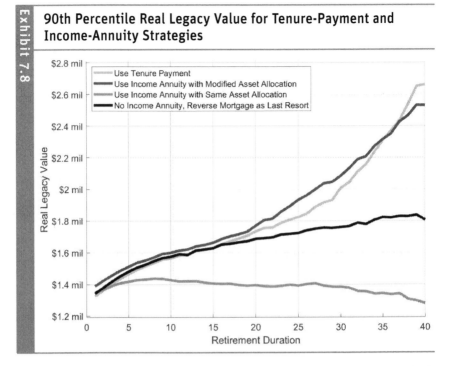

Exhibit 7.8

90th Percentile Real Legacy Value for Tenure-Payment and Income-Annuity Strategies

with the income annuity using the modified-asset-allocation strategy. Both strategies help to keep more invested in the markets at a time when they do well, and they provide more relief for portfolio withdrawals, allowing more assets to remain in the portfolio for growth. The no-income-annuity option falls next in the ranking of outcomes, since this strategy also allows more to remain in the market when markets have done well. Finally, the income-annuity option with the same asset allocation removes the most growth potential for the portfolio and leaves the relative smallest amount of legacy at the ninetieth percentile of the distribution.

Further Reading

Consumer Financial Protection Bureau. 2017. "Issue Brief: The Costs and Risks of Using a Reverse Mortgage to Delay Collecting Social Security."

Tomlinson, Joseph. 2015. "New Research: Reverse Mortgages, SPIAs and Retirement Income." *Advisor Perspectives* (April 14).

Tomlinson, Joseph, Shaun Pfeiffer, and John Salter. 2016. "Reverse Mortgages, Annuities, and Investments: Sorting Out the Options to Generate Sustainable Retirement Income." *Journal of Personal Finance* 15 (1): 27–36.

CHAPTER 8

Preserve Credit as an "Insurance" Policy

The final use for a reverse mortgage is to preserve the line of credit as an insurance policy against a variety of retirement risks. Preserving credit as insurance involves setting up a HECM reverse mortgage as early as possible and then leaving it unused until needed. The up-front costs for the reverse mortgage could be treated as an insurance premium that may never need to be used if everything else goes well in retirement. However, a variety of potential pitfalls face retirees, and implementing a reverse mortgage earlier in retirement could support a sizeable pool of contingency assets.

I have already discussed one aspect of this insurance protection in chapter 6, in which a line of credit is opened and then used to support retirement spending only in the event of portfolio depletion. In this regard, the insurance provided by the HECM is against market losses that risk the ability to meet retirement-portfolio distribution goals. This was one of six strategies to coordinate portfolio spending with home equity. In this edition of the book, the slower growth of the line of credit reduces the strategy's competitiveness with other coordinated strategies, but it does remain as a viable option.

Another aspect of the insurance that could be provided by a HECM line of credit is to treat it as a large contingency fund to help meet unplanned expenses. For example, a reverse mortgage could help as part of a divorce settlement. In this scenario, the reverse mortgage could allow one ex-spouse to stay in the home, with the reverse mortgage used to pay a necessary portion of the home's equity to the other ex-spouse. Alternatively, the home could be sold with the proceeds split, and then each of the ex-spouses could use his or her half of the home equity with a HECM for Purchase to obtain a home of similar value to the original. The line of credit could also be used to support in-home care or other health expenses to avoid or delay institutional living in the face of long-term care needs.

The focus of this chapter is a final insurance aspect that requires a bit more explanation: using the HECM as a way to protect the value of your home. With the current HECM rules, those living in their homes long enough could reap a windfall when the line of credit exceeds the home's value. This potential windfall is amplified by today's low interest rates. Even if the value of the home declines, the line of credit will continue to grow without regard for the home's subsequent value. Though this strategy remains, I will explain how the updated rules from October 2017 have dramatically reduced the likelihood for this strategy to create benefits for newly issued loans.

Combining the principal limit with the fact that a HECM is a nonrecourse loan means that the HECM provides a valuable hedging property for home prices. What is the specific probability that the value of a standby line of credit will grow to exceed the home value? I have sought to answer this by simulating future home prices and future one-month LIBOR rates that will guide the growth of the line of credit. With each of these values projected over time, we can determine how frequently a line of credit may exceed the value of the home across a large number of simulated futures.

For this example, I assume the borrowers are sixty-two years old, the ten-year LIBOR swap rate is 2.25 percent, the current one-month LIBOR rate is 1.25 percent, the lender's margin is 2.25 percent, and up-front costs will be financed from the investment portfolio. This combination results in an expected rate of 4.5 percent and a principal limit factor of 43.9 percent.

The initial effective rate is 4 percent (1.25 percent LIBOR, 2.25 percent lender's margin, and 0.5 percent mortgage-insurance premium). If interest rates never rose, it would take far too long for a 1 percent spread in the growth rate (4 percent less 3 percent for an assumed home-value growth rate) to allow the line of credit, which is initially 43.9 percent of the home value, to grow and surpass the home value. But if we forecast one-month LIBOR rates to gradually increase in the future, the increased variable rates for the HECM line of credit improve the odds for the principal limit to eventually exceed a randomly fluctuating home price.

Exhibit 8.1 shows the probabilities that the HECM line of credit has grown to exceed the home's value for a sixty-two-year-old borrower. With these simulations, there is a 50 percent chance of this by age ninety-four and the potential to obtain a windfall from the line of credit, since it represents a nonrecourse loan. This serves as protection, especially when the value of the home declines during retirement.

For the applicable rules for loans issued before October 2017, I previously reported that this median break-even age was eighty-one, so the new rules have increased the age by thirteen years—reducing the odds that retirees will benefit from the strategy. When considered with the increased up-front costs for reverse mortgages triggered by the new rules, I do not expect many retirees to open reverse mortgages now with a primary intention of treating the HECM as a protection on the value of their home.

A few caveats of this strategy to hedge home prices with the HECM are worth discussing. First, these probabilities may actually be underestimated, because any given home may experience more price volatility than the overall Case-Shiller index for home prices. David Blanchett has estimated the volatility of individual homes at double the level of overall home price

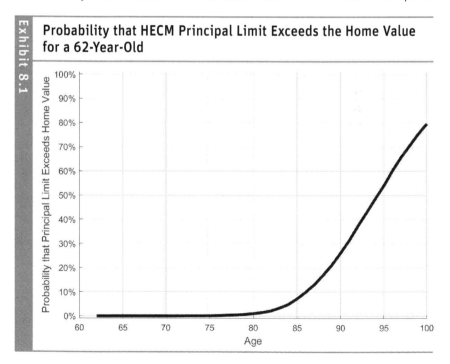

Exhibit 8.1

Probability that HECM Principal Limit Exceeds the Home Value for a 62-Year-Old

indices used in these simulations. Individual homes are at more risk of experiencing substantial price declines relative to the index, creating more opportunity for the hedging value to be realized. The line of credit becomes valuable in cases when the home price falls. In financial language, it is essentially a "put option" on the value of the home. The line of credit can provide a positive net payment when the home value declines.

Second, there is an important aspect of timing the decision about when to access the line of credit. The longer you wait, the greater the potential growth for the pot of funds that can be obtained. Generally, the principal limit, loan balance, and line of credit grow at the same rate. But for any loan balance, the growth reflects the growing interest and mortgage premiums due rather than growing access to new funds. Waiting is advantageous, but if you wait too long and suddenly die, it's too late and the line of credit is no longer available. Estates and nonborrowing spouses cannot take advantage of the windfall after the sudden death of the borrower. It is best not to become too greedy once a windfall has developed from the nonrecourse aspects of the HECM program.

Finally, to be clear, this use of a HECM line of credit as home-value protection can be considered a "loophole" in the current program. Opening a reverse mortgage and then not using it works against the interests of some lenders and the government's mortgage-insurance fund. The lender is not able to charge interest, which could create real difficulties for lenders that have reduced up-front costs by providing a higher margin and have paid a commission to the loan originator. Also, the mortgage-insurance fund is unable to collect further premiums to support coverage of any shortfall to the lender when the borrower gets more out of the home than it is worth. This surely explains part of the justification for the government to close a large portion of this "loophole" for new loans issued since October 2017.

With this approach, borrowers may also be encouraged in subtle ways to let the value of their home decline so that they can make a smaller repayment. Thus, while this option is available today—and I could say that it is even encouraged with the heightened government efforts to reduce the speed at which borrowers use up their lines of credit—I expect that the government will eventually work to further weaken or eliminate this hedging opportunity.

As new businesses are increasingly able to offer real-time estimates of home value, one possibility for future borrowers is that the borrowing capacity will be capped at the appraised home value. Another possibility is that the government could begin to charge the mortgage-insurance premium on the value of the principal limit rather than on the loan balance. This would vastly increase the cost of the insurance strategy, possibly overturning its value completely. However, for the time being, these insurance opportunities exist within the current HECM program.

Further Reading

Blanchett, David. 2017. "The Home as a Risky Asset." *Journal of Personal Finance* 16 (1): 7–28.

CHAPTER 9

Determining If a HECM Reverse Mortgage Is Right for You

In the previous chapters, I sought to provide context for how a retirement-income strategy can extend beyond traditional wealth management to better manage the many risks of retirement. Namely, I discussed a variety of ways that a strategic plan for home equity can be a beneficial part of a retirement-income plan.

This final chapter is more about the process of deciding on whether a HECM is right for you. I will answer some of the key frequently asked questions I have received since publishing the first edition of this book. I'll also look in more detail at the risks associated with a reverse mortgage and provide tips on how to find a reverse-mortgage lender. I will conclude with a summary of matters to keep in mind and a brief discussion about next steps for finding additional help or education on retirement topics.

◉ Reverse-Mortgage Risks

A common thought upon first learning about the HECM program is that it seems almost too good to be true and that there must be a catch involved. I am often asked about reverse-mortgage risks. I summarize here their potential risks so that the discussion is clear, making it easier for readers to analyze the costs and benefits of a variable-rate HECM.

Program Complexities Can Lead to Misunderstandings

When discussing reverse-mortgage risks, the first matter to emphasize is that many of the commonly mentioned risks involve misunderstandings on the part of borrowers or heirs about how the program works. In 2015, the Consumer Finance Protection Bureau published two reports about reverse mortgages that describe risks and complaints about the program. First, their "Snapshot of Reverse Mortgage Complaints: December 2011–December 2014" was released in February 2015. It notes that for the three-year period investigated, reverse-mortgage complaints represent about 1 percent of the mortgage complaints received by the CFPB and that the reverse-mortgage market size is about 1 percent of the total mortgage market. Thus, there is not a disproportionate number of complaints about reverse mortgages.

After reading this book, you should recognize that many of the complaints discussed in the CFPB report stem from misunderstandings on the part of those lodging them. Nonetheless, these complaints do allow us to reflect again on some of the complicated features of the HECM program and the misunderstandings they may generate.

The most common complaint category (38 percent of complaints) relates to problems when someone is unable to pay, such as a borrower's desire to refinance a loan when home equity is insufficient to do so. Borrowers also complain about being unable to change loan terms, like seeking to lower interest rates or the lender's margin, or feeling that the variable-rate portion of the effective rate has risen too quickly. Borrowers also complain about not being able to add additional borrowers to the loan in order to avoid the loan balance becoming due. For instance, adult children complain about not being able to be added to the loan as borrowers or at least to become eligible nonborrowers. As well, nonborrowing spouses have complained about not being able to be added as borrowers after the loan has commenced.

Due to the actuarial nature of the program and how the principal limit factors are determined, it should be clear to readers that these types of requests are not allowed and not reasonable. Having more younger borrowers added to the loan would increase the time to loan maturity and would require a lower initial principal limit factor than already provided. As well, for the case of nonborrowing spouses, the protections for eligible nonborrowing spouses were added near the end of the period under review (August 4, 2014), which should at least reduce these types of complaints. Nonborrowing spouses must remember, though, that they are not borrowers and will not be able to continue to access funds from the line of credit once the borrower has left the home.

In 2014, the Consumer Financial Protection Bureau conducted focus-group studies in which consumers were shown advertisements about reverse mortgages and asked for their perceptions. They provided the results of this investigation in a June 2015 report entitled, "A Closer Look at Reverse Mortgage Advertisements and Consumer Risks." Some of those in the focus group did not understand that a reverse mortgage would have to be repaid in the future, or that there are fees or interest involved. Rather, they viewed it as a type of welfare program directly administered by the federal government. Others viewed the loan balance as a way to spend home equity, not understanding the mechanism whereby this would reduce the value of their share of home equity in the future. Still others thought that the "tax-free" nature of reverse mortgages would mean that property taxes would no longer have to be paid. Others misunderstood explanations about those able to stay in the home as their not being subject to any of the eligibility requirements for the loan. The explanation of reverse mortgages in chapter 4, hopefully, means that you well understand these aspects.

Dealing with the Reverse-Mortgage Loan-Servicing Companies

The one area of complaints in the CFPB report that readers should remain wary about relates to loan servicing. Consumers have complained that servicers can make it difficult to coordinate repayment, may act as if property taxes and other homeowner obligations have not been met and improperly try to foreclose on a loan, do not maintain accurate records (or even lose important documents), and are unresponsive to communications. As well, when the loan balance becomes due, some have complained of appraisers inflating home values to force a higher payoff amount when the nonrecourse aspects of the loan are in effect. Since the loan balance continues to grow with interest until repayment is made, delays in this area also have the effect of increasing the subsequent amount due.

One example I have personally witnessed is of a reader who obtained a reverse mortgage and then experienced hail damage to the roof of the home. The homeowner's insurance provided a check to repair the roof but made it out to both the homeowner and the reverse-mortgage servicing company. The reverse-mortgage servicer was very unresponsive and

FINRA's Stance on Reverse Mortgages

FINRA is the Financial Industry Regulatory Authority. It is a self-regulatory body for financial brokers and brokerage firms. As a part of its efforts to protect consumers, it issues alerts and reports on a variety of financial issues, including reverse mortgages. FINRA's stance on them is described in a report entitled, "Reverse Mortgages: Avoiding a Reversal of Fortune." This is a cute and clever title that clearly casts negative connotations on these mortgages, leading many financial advisors and financial broker-dealer firms who receive guidance from FINRA to conclude that reverse mortgages are a bad idea and do not allow their affiliated financial advisors to discuss reverse mortgages with their customers.

However, while its title has not changed, the report itself has evolved over the years. It used to tell investors to consider reverse mortgages only as a last-resort option, but after Barry Sacks published his research (discussed in chapter 6), he convinced FINRA to remove that language.

The current version of the report provides three reasons to be cautious about reverse mortgages. Readers of chapter 4 should be familiar with these matters. First, FINRA warns that reverse mortgages may "seem like 'free money' but in fact, they can be quite expensive." The report mentions the up-front costs and ongoing interest on the loan balance.

Second, the report mentions that reverse mortgages must be the primary mortgage on the home. This is not really a reason to be cautious, but the report points out that after paying off an existing mortgage from the initial principal limit, borrowers may have less access to cash than they had anticipated.

Next, the report reminds investors that they are still responsible for property taxes, insurance, and home-maintenance costs. Finally, the report reminds borrowers that the loan will become due should they decide to move out of the home. With accumulated interest, borrowers might be surprised about the amount of home equity that they have left after repaying the loan.

The report then reminds borrowers to use the loan wisely rather than for frivolous expenses. As this book has focused on using home equity as part of a responsible retirement-income plan, hopefully, this point is clear already. Nonetheless, it is worth providing a quotation from the report that drives home this point: "Those same homeowners may need their home equity some day for something far more pressing than a vacation, only to find that it has already been spent."

The report ends with some tips when considering reverse mortgages. First, weigh all your options. Besides a reverse mortgage, other options include selling one's house to downsize or rent, using a home-equity line of credit, or seeking local-government assistance to help cover property taxes and home maintenance. Next, understand the costs and fees of the loan. Third, recognize the full impact of the reverse mortgage, such as the impact of loan proceeds on state and federal benefits such as Medicaid.

This section continues with the sentence, "Finally, a reverse mortgage is generally not the right choice for those who want to leave their homes to their heirs." However, this language probably should also have been removed following the implications of Barry Sacks's research. Since money is fungible, the report's statement is wrong when coordinated strategies can create synergies for the investment portfolio to manage sequence risk that leads to a larger overall legacy after repaying any loan balance.

The next FINRA tip is to obtain independent advice through loan counseling, particularly if one is considering a proprietary reverse mortgage that is not part of the HECM program. Finally, its last two points are about being skeptical about using reverse mortgages as a way to fund an investment or insurance product. I hope I have been clear that this is not a valid use of a reverse mortgage. I have discussed coordinating the reverse mortgage with an existing portfolio or using a reverse mortgage to continue to pay premiums on an existing long-term care policy, but I have not suggested that a reverse mortgage be used to fund new investment or insurance products.

uncooperative about endorsing the check so that it could be cashed and the roof could be repaired.

Fortunately, in this case, the reverse-mortgage lender who had initiated the loan stepped in and worked with the servicer to make sure that the right actions were taken. The lender was not obligated to help with this; it may, however, indicate that working with someone locally (rather than remotely, through a call center) can be important for getting help with future servicing issues. It may be worth paying a bit more in up-front costs to work with someone who can serve as a trustworthy advocate in this area. Choosing a servicer for a reverse mortgage is no guarantee, though, because just like with traditional mortgages, these loans are traded, and you may end up with a quite different servicer than you expect.

Temptations to Use Irresponsibly

Another risk for reverse mortgages relates to the fact that spending down home equity does mean that less of it will be available later in retirement. Any outstanding loan balance on a reverse mortgage grows with interest over time. Borrowers must understand this point.

Creating liquidity for home equity with a reverse mortgage can allow for more strategic retirement-income plans that better protect against retirement sequence risk for portfolio distributions. But there is always a temptation to overspend when the money is available. For those who might look at a reverse mortgage as a means to overspend, this could jeopardize the ability to meet spending obligations later in retirement. Such individuals may be better off keeping their home equity illiquid and thereby avoid misusing the potential benefits of liquidity.

For those who incorporate reverse mortgages as part of a responsible overall plan and don't use the home equity on unnecessary luxuries, this risk is not relevant. But it remains a risk for those without adequate self-control.

Qualifying for Means-Tested Benefits

Proceeds from a reverse mortgage can be described as "tax free" in the sense that these cash flows do not count as part of the adjusted gross income for determining income taxes. However, spending from a reverse mortgage, or holding some reverse-mortgage proceeds in a bank account, could reduce eligibility for means-tested benefits like Supplemental Security Income or Medicaid. For those thinking about reverse mortgages as a "last-resort" option, it is important to consider the potential impact of the reverse mortgage on other government benefits.

Destruction of the Home through Natural Disasters

A common question I receive relates to what happens to the reverse mortgage if a home is destroyed through earthquake, flood, fire, and the like. Generally, the homeowner has sufficient insurance coverage to rebuild the home on the same property, and the disaster event will not trigger the loan balance to become due. However, the loan balance could become due if one has insufficient insurance coverage to rebuild or decides to move to a new location because it is impossible to rebuild on the same property.

The risk here is that the loan balance could become due sooner than the borrower had expected. For those with sufficient remaining assets, this could be a nuisance but not necessarily a severe disruption for the success of the retirement plan.

But this risk can be particularly problematic for those using a reverse mortgage as a last-resort option once other assets deplete. An extreme example of this risk took place in Oregon in 2012, when a woman in her eighties had her home taken through eminent domain to allow a highway expansion through her area. The woman had already spent the proceeds from the reverse mortgage and had enough income to continue maintaining the obligations to stay in her home. But while the eminent-domain action compensated her for the value of the home, the money had to be used to repay the loan balance on the reverse mortgage, because she could no longer live on the property and was no longer eligible. In this case, the unexpected need to repay the reverse-mortgage loan because of the eminent-domain action essentially left her homeless. Any natural disaster that requires a move from the original property could essentially have the same impact.

For those without other options, it is important to also consider what the alternatives would have been without the reverse mortgage. While the situation is bad when one can unexpectedly no longer live in the home, this type of outcome might simply have occurred even earlier in the absence of the reverse mortgage. With this risk, it is not clear that a reverse mortgage was a bad idea, unless it was being used simply to fund frivolous expenses.

The Maximum Mortgage Amount

Reverse-mortgage contracts need inherent limits on how long they last and on how much can be borrowed. They cannot be limitless. The higher the limits, the higher the demand on the mortgage-insurance fund and the larger the payments for the mortgage-insurance premiums. In states where these limits must be specified, the constraints are generally to age 150 and to a maximum mortgage amount of 150 percent of the eligible home value when the HECM begins. For instance, if a home is appraised at $600,000 for the purposes of initiating the HECM, then the maximum mortgage amount is $900,000.

Though borrowers are unlikely to find the age limit binding, it is possible for the principal limit to grow to the size of the maximum mortgage amount, especially for loans made under the pre-October 2017 rule change. What happens when the principal limit reaches this limit?

The consensus within the reverse-mortgage industry is that lenders will allow the borrower to sign paperwork to modify the loan documents to further extend the maximum mortgage amount, ensuring that the disbursements from the line of credit can continue even if this would push the loan balance above the maximum mortgage amount set in the original contract. Though it will be necessary to revisit the reverse mortgage with additional paperwork at that time, the common expectation is that lenders will be willing to coordinate the allowance of further disbursements from the loan beyond the original limit.

It should be noted that not everyone in the reverse-mortgage world expects this to proceed so smoothly. For those whose principal limit includes a substantial loan-balance component, the process is likely to operate as anticipated. But a caveat should be made that those considering to take the "ruthless option" for the reverse mortgage, which is to open a reverse mortgage line of credit and to then let it sit unused for decades with the hope that one day, the line of credit will grow larger than the value of the home and provide a windfall due to the loan's nonrecourse aspects.

This strategy, which I discussed in chapter 8, is still quite rare in practice and requires staying in the home for decades. It is plausible that in such cases, lenders will be unwilling to modify the loan documents, which could mean that disbursements from the line of credit cannot exceed the maximum mortgage amount. It may be rare that this ever becomes an issue, but if it happens, the line of credit's growth would remain capped at 150 percent of the eligible home value from when the loan began rather than continue without any limit. This should be viewed as a potential risk for strategies that open a HECM line of credit and potentially leave it unused for decades.

◉ Finding a High-Quality Reverse-Mortgage Lender

Another common question I receive regards how to find a trustworthy reverse-mortgage lender. This is not necessarily easy for those beginning the process with little more to rely on than an Internet search engine. A starting point may be with personal referrals from your financial advisor, or from friends or family who have felt satisfied with their lenders. I am also willing to help readers find the names of local lenders from reputable companies if you write to me providing your city and state. I am not compensated by reverse-mortgage lenders for giving such referrals.

It is important to speak with a few different lenders and to get a sense of the range of possibilities with regard to reverse-mortgage options in terms of up-front costs, the lender's margin, and ongoing costs, and whether the lender can serve as a resource to address any servicing issues after the loan is initiated. Costs will vary and can depend on how the loan is used: those wishing to set up a line of credit as a later resource may have to pay a higher up-front cost than those who plan to spend more quickly from the HECM. It is important to consider more than just who offers the lowest up-front costs, because having a personal connection to the lender can be important for any subsequent servicing issues or questions, and because the interaction of up-front costs and the lender's margin can be complicated and hard to assess.

Here are some issues to consider when speaking with a lender:

- Is the lender patient about meeting with you in person or speaking by phone to answer your questions?
- Is the lender clear about the different terms and costs available for reverse mortgages? Does he or she explain the costs clearly and not try to hide them by emphasizing only the possibility of no "out-of-pocket" costs?
- Has the lender been clear about your responsibilities regarding property taxes, maintaining homeowner's insurance, and keeping the property maintained?
- Has the lender suggested that you seek additional guidance for tax advice or for advice about receiving assistance from government-welfare programs, if relevant?
- Does the lender demonstrate interest or knowledge about retirement-income planning so that you have a better sense about the right options and strategies for your situation? Is the lender conversant about the topics and issues raised in this book?

As well, there are some red flags to consider that may suggest that a lender is not the right choice for you:

- The lender pressures you to make a decision about applying for a reverse mortgage before you feel comfortable or ready.
- The lender encourages you to take a larger proceed from the line of credit when the loan begins than you otherwise feel comfortable with or feel is necessary for your situation.
- The lender encourages you to use the reverse-mortgage proceeds to buy a new investment or insurance product, especially if it seems as though the lender could receive some sort of compensation if you do.
- The lender provides you with a list of HUD-approved independent counselors, as it should, but tries to direct you to a specific counselor.

◎ Final Thoughts and Seeking Further Help

We have covered a lot of ground. I first introduced retirement-income planning and the new risks of retirement to provide a context and framework for thinking about how home equity could be integrated into a retirement-income strategy. I then described the variable-rate HECM option in detail, along with assessments of different strategies for using the HECM and how they compare with other possibilities. We found value in incorporating HECMs early on as part of an overall strategy rather than treating them as a last-resort option for later in retirement. We then considered the risks to keep in mind about reverse mortgages and some tips about finding a good lender to work with.

At present, reverse mortgages are underutilized by the US population. Since the beginnings of the HECM program, more than one million loans have been initiated, and the FHA reports that there were 560,023 outstanding HECM loans at the end of September 2017. Mark Warshawsky reports that in 2015, there were about thirty-six million US households with someone aged at least sixty-two, and roughly 1.6 percent of these are using HECMs. He estimates, however, that about 12 to 14 percent of these households are suitable candidates for HECMs: their homes are eligible, have mortgages of less than 40 percent of the home's value, and could generate at least 10 percent more overall retirement income with a HECM. So, there is still plenty of room for growth with the HECM program.

If you are thinking to use a reverse mortgage in retirement, it's important to first ensure that you are eligible. Is there a potential borrower who is at least sixty-two? Is the home used as the primary residence? Does the borrower plan on living in the home for a least long enough to make it worthwhile to pay the up-front costs for setting up the reverse mortgage? Is there an existing mortgage on the home that is small enough to either be paid off with other assets and/or refinanced through the credit available with the reverse mortgage?

If so, then it is important to reflect on whether the HECM provides the best option and how it may be used. The National Reverse Mortgage Lenders Association provides a reverse-mortgage self-evaluation checklist of questions; I've drawn on it for these:

- How do you intend to use the reverse mortgage?
- Is there any other use for home equity that might work better?
- Would a reverse mortgage disrupt eligibility for other government-welfare programs such as Supplemental Security Income or Medicaid?

- How long do you plan to stay in your current home?
- Do you fully understand the costs and homeowner obligations?
- Who will be the borrower? Are there any eligible nonborrowing spouses? Are there any ineligible nonborrowers who will be on the home title?
- How do you anticipate repaying any loan balance when the reverse mortgage becomes due?

My hope is that this book will help you structure answers to these questions, especially regarding how you intend to use the reverse mortgage.

Seeking Further Help

There are several options for readers who seek additional education or help beyond what I've provided here.

For those nearing retirement and wishing to delegate some of the responsibilities around managing finances for retirement income, I serve as a principal at McLean Asset Management (www.mcleanam.com). McLean is a fee-only, fiduciary financial-planning firm that truly understands the retirement-income problem and is ready to help you. You can contact me at wade@retirementresearcher.com if you would like to set up a short introductory call with an advisor at McLean.

For readers preferring a do-it-yourself approach, my www. RetirementResearcher.com website provides independent, data-driven, and research-based information about retirement-income planning. The website is geared toward providing unbiased information about building efficient retirement-income strategies and is willing to cross between the various silos of the financial-services profession. My aim for the website is to empower readers about retirement-income planning and further expand into other areas important for an effective retirement. I want the site to act as a clearinghouse of knowledge to be digested at the reader's own pace. At the website, you can sign up for a weekly newsletter on retirement topics.

Finally, for financial advisors and reverse-mortgage professionals, I serve as a professor of retirement income at The American College of Financial Services. We are the home of the Retirement Income Certified

Professional (RICP) designation. The college has made the relatively new field of retirement income into a top priority for the future. We now also serve as the home of the Funding Longevity Task Force, which has the stated purpose to develop and advance an objective understanding of the role that housing wealth can play in retirement-income planning. It was the Task Force that first sparked my interest in reverse mortgages a few years ago.

Further Reading

Consumer Financial Protection Bureau. 2015. "Snapshot of Reverse Mortgage Complaints; December 2011–December 2014."

Consumer Financial Protection Bureau. 2015. "A Closer Look at Reverse Mortgage Advertisements and Consumer Risks."

Financial Industry Regulatory Authority. 2014. "Reverse Mortgages: Avoiding a Reversal of Fortune." Investor Education Series.

Murguia, Alex. "What McLean Can Do For You." McLean E-book Series. https://www.mcleanam.com/resources/

Warshawsky, Mark J. 2017. "Retire on the House: The Possible Use of Reverse Mortgages to Enhance Retirement Security." Mercatus Working Paper.

GLOSSARY OF ACRONYMS

- AARP – American Association of Retired Persons
- AGI – adjusted gross income
- ALF – assisted living facility
- CCRC – continuing-care retirement community
- CD – certificate of deposit
- CEO – chief executive officer
- CFP – Certified Financial Planner
- CLU – Chartered Life Underwriter
- DIA – deferred-income annuities
- FHA – Federal Housing Authority
- FPA – Financial Planning Association
- HECM – home-equity conversion mortgage
- HELOC – home-equity line of credit
- HUD – Department of Housing and Urban Development
- IRA – individual retirement account
- IRS – Internal Revenue Service
- LESA – life-expectancy set-aside
- LIBOR – London Interbank Offered Rate
- LOC – line of credit
- MIP – mortgage-insurance premium
- MPT – modern portfolio theory
- NAPFA – National Association for Personal Financial Advisors
- PLF – principal limit factor
- RIA – registered investment adviser
- RICP – Retirement Income Certified Professional
- SPIA – single-premium immediate annuities
- TIPS – Treasury inflation-protected securities

ABOUT THE AUTHOR

Wade D. Pfau, PhD, CFA, is a professor of retirement income in the PhD program for Financial and Retirement Planning at The American College of Financial Services in Bryn Mawr, Pennsylvania. He also serves as a principal and the director of retirement research for McLean Asset Management and chief planning scientist at inStream Solutions. He hosts the Retirement Researcher website as an educational resource for individuals and financial advisors on topics related to retirement-income planning. He holds a doctorate in economics from Princeton University and publishes frequently in a wide variety of academic and practitioner research journals.

In 2016, he was chosen as part of the inaugural Icons and Innovators award class by InvestmentNews. Other professional recognition includes serving as a past selectee for the *InvestmentNews* "Power 20" in 2013 and "40 Under 40" in 2014, the Investment Advisor 35 list for 2015 and 25 list for 2014, and *Financial Planning* magazine's Influencer Awards in 2012. He is a two-time winner of the *Journal of Financial Planning's* Montgomery-Warschauer Editor's Award, a two-time winner of the Academic Thought Leadership Award from the Retirement Income Industry Association, and a best-paper award winner in the retirement category from the Academy of Financial Services.

He has spoken at the national conferences of organizations such as the CFA Institute, Financial Planning Association, National Association of Personal Financial Advisors, and the Academy of Financial Services.

He is also a contributor to the curriculum of the Retirement Income Certified Professional (RICP) designation for financial advisors. He is a coeditor of the *Journal of Personal Finance*. Wade is also a columnist for *Advisor Perspectives*, a contributor to Forbes, and an expert panelist for the *Wall Street Journal*. His research has been discussed in outlets including the print editions of *The Economist, New York Times, Wall Street Journal*, Time, Kiplinger's, and *Money Magazine*.

He is the author of the books *How Much Can I Spend in Retirement? A Guide to Investment-Based Retirement Income Strategies* and *Reverse Mortgages: How to Use Reverse Mortgages to Secure Your Retirement*.

INDEX

Made in the USA
Lexington, KY
24 July 2019